URBAN FORMALISM

POLIS: Fordham Series in Urban Studies
Edited by Daniel J. Monti, Saint Louis University

POLIS will address the questions of what makes a good community and how urban dwellers succeed and fail to live up to the idea that people from various backgrounds and levels of society can live together effectively, if not always congenially. The series is the province of no single discipline; we are searching for authors in fields as diverse as American studies, anthropology, history, political science, sociology, and urban studies who can write for both academic and informed lay audiences. Our objective is to celebrate and critically assess the customary ways in which urbanites make the world corrigible for themselves and the other kinds of people with whom they come into contact every day.

To this end, we will publish both book-length manuscripts and a series of "digital shorts" (e-books) focusing on case studies of groups, locales, and events that provide clues as to how urban people accomplish this delicate and exciting task. We expect to publish one or two books every year but a larger number of "digital shorts." The digital shorts will be 20,000 words or fewer and have a strong narrative voice.

Urban
Formalism

THE WORK OF CITY READING

David Faflik

FORDHAM UNIVERSITY PRESS   NEW YORK 2020

Fordham University Press has no responsibility for the
persistence or accuracy of URLs for external or third-
party Internet websites referred to in this publication and
does not guarantee that any content on such websites is,
or will remain, accurate or appropriate.

Fordham University Press also publishes its books in a
variety of electronic formats. Some content that appears
in print may not be available in electronic books.
Visit us online at www.fordhampress.com.

Library of Congress Cataloging-in-Publication Data
available online at https://catalog.loc.gov.

Printed in the United States of America

22 21 20   5 4 3 2 1

First edition

Contents

URBAN FORMALISM

Introduction

The form of a city changes faster, alas! Than a
mortal heart

—CHARLES BAUDELAIRE, "THE SWAN"

This book rests upon a pair of related propositions that have far-reaching consequences for the work of urban studies. The first is that the history of the modern city is a history of urban forms. The second is that the interpretive turn to *formalism* represents a wholly new approach to thinking about urbanism and historicism. In other words, this book argues that to conceive of the city "formally" is not only to revise our understanding of the city's actual existence. It is to argue for an alternative way of apprehending the conditions through which knowledge of the city is even possible. Forms alter our sense of what the historical city *was*. Forms change how we perceive the very practice of urban perception, whether we're talking about the perceptual habits of historical observers from the past or anyone who is mindful, today, of how forms function in the present century. In the final analysis, the twin claims on which this book depends suggest a different kind of urban *being* even as they propose a novel approach to city "reading." In forms, we'll never know the city the same way again.

By *formalism*, I mean something other than the old standby set of interpretive strategies by which we've typically accounted for those classical aesthetic properties (including elements of line, shape, color, texture, and composition) that have long served as signposts for whatever many of us may have been conditioned to regard as "artful."[1] I would similarly liberate the discussion of *urban* forms from the postwar preoccupation with plastic "images" that informs such noteworthy investigations of the city as Kevin Lynch's writings on formal archetypes like paths, edges, districts, nodes, and landmarks.[2] Instead, I deploy the term *formalism* in a way that's meant to change how we regard cities *as* cities, while challenging us to travel down what is probably an unfamiliar route to attaining urban knowledge. First, I contend that during the period that is the focus of this study — the pivotal phase of urban development in the West, the early to middle decades of the nineteenth century — the city was itself the repository of countless forms in its very makeup; each of these could be made sense of by someone who was ready to recognize the formal patterns that emerged as urban life simply unfolded. Second, I maintain that even the decipherers of cities — city "readers," we'll call them, as is now customary in the interdisciplinary field of urban cultural studies — who'd received no special formal instruction were potentially as well equipped as anyone else to decode the forms (and the relations between forms) from which their urban milieu in the North Atlantic world was built.[3] City peoples would have found forms just about everywhere they turned in these years. Some of these forms were familiar, as were the architectural styles, neighborhood squares, traffic flows, foodways, folkways, dress preferences, and hum and hustle of commercial life that defined the look and layout and feel of cities as the century progressed. Other forms were less apparent yet likewise rich with meaning. These included the location and formation of racial and ethnic enclaves; the assigning of gender roles; the length and pace of the workday; and the rate and range of the spread of municipal services like water, sewage, and garbage collection. On its own, any one of these forms — whether attributable to time, space, built surfaces, or lived practices — was indicative of a city teeming with countless ways of being comprehended. Together, these forms were an open invitation for readers to absorb the staggering size and scale and variety of the city by attending to the patterns (regular or irregular, repeatable or random, obvious or inconspicuous) that gave meaning to the surrounding cityscape, if one were predisposed to look.

The appeal of a formal model of city reading is at least twofold. It is reflexive enough, to begin, to encourage a certain self-awareness among even the most casual of urban observers. When we make a study of the respective levels of responsiveness demonstrated by others, we cannot help but take stock of just how responsive we are to the city. As a means of reading, additionally, formalism was and remains an accommodating enough interpretive framework to reflect the wide range of registers — sweeping and panoramic on the one hand, up close and personal on the other — in which the formally minded readers who concern us operated. This last point is crucial. For in positing a mutually constitutive relation between formalism, urbanism, and historicism, I am not just advancing a newfangled way to fathom the city as an isolated construct. I am advocating, rather, an interpretive practice that proceeds from a more holistic understanding of the urban than has been conventional even in a globalizing age such as ours. That is to say,

I'm arguing that the interpretive use of forms is not only historically "true" because it affords us a flexible way to gauge
the lives of our urban predecessors; it is also strategic, in that
it makes allowances for a theoretical conception of the urban that moves beyond the narrowly "atomistic" manner in
which David Harvey says too many previous commentators
have framed the city.[4]

"Most writers," Harvey explains, "seem to agree that the
city has to be regarded as a functioning totality within which
everything is related to everything else" (*Social Justice and
the City*, 303). At the same time, Harvey and Edward Soja
concur (on the general reductive tendencies of city reading, if not on the particular habits it entails in practice) that
the interpretations we share of the urban represent at best
a partial account of modernity, from the start of the nineteenth century forward. For example, certain members of
a scientific subset of sociologists, economists, geographers,
architects, and city planners have derived their sense of
the urban by attending almost exclusively to the social processes they associate with the city. Others discover in what
Soja calls the domains of the "temporal/historical" or the
"spatial/geographical" an equally compelling, and equally
delimiting, location from which to draw their conclusions
about the urban, writ large.[5] But whether city readers betray a preference for what Harvey names the sociological
or geographical "imagination" (*Social Justice and the City*,
23) or else favor the "historicality" that Soja insists has made
observers of the urban more receptive to time than space
(*Seeking Spatial Justice*, 70), they often ignore their own as-
sumptions about the integrative forces that give animating
life to cities. Not even the "demographic imagination" that
Nicholas Haly says "emerged within modern culture as populations exploded" across national borders, on either side of
the nineteenth-century Atlantic, fully captures the collective

quality of the urban consciousness that I'd claim as the necessary interpretive correlative when- and wherever we read
the city *formally*, as a repository of interrelated forms.[6]

Formalism hardly amounts to a grand unified theory of
the city. Forms do, however, afford us a vantage from which
to better appreciate the infinite variety and diversity of urban conditions, which are always encompassing and only
ever changing. By way of illustration, the "subtle and complex formal patterns" that Caroline Levine interrogates in
her book *Forms* (2015) speak not only to the fact that forms
impart legibility as much to the social as to the more strictly
aesthetic dimensions of our lives. They are also a reminder
that forms enable us to read *in between*, to draw connections among such assorted aspects of modern life as might
otherwise seem separate, disparate, disconnected. Levine's
forms — she counts "wholes," "rhythms," "hierarchies," and
"networks" among the historical and current "patterns" she
examines — help "structure everyday experience" without
lending default support to the overwhelming urge toward
order (or conversely, the postmodern slide toward fracture)
that many a student of the nineteenth century has long associated with the disciplinary regimens of modernity. Forms
for Levine may or may not be marked by the neat finish
of "high" literature, the exalted polish of museum art, or
the rationalized, standardizing effects of protoindustrial-
ism. What chiefly characterizes such forms as figure into
her readings of time intervals, the configurations of social
groups, the recurrence of images and numeric sequences,
and the unlooked-for appearance of ranked pairs is that they
are recognizable enough at face value to suggest patterns yet
random enough to retain that essence of comparative unpre-
dictability and difference which we identify with the "everyday." In making a case for the free play of culture, Levine
subscribes to a practical formalism which, instead of helping

us achieve a modicum of coherence in our existence, en-
ables us to cultivate a mindset of responsiveness that's open
to the heterogeneity of what she calls "ordinary life." This
last is the cultural space within which urban formalists have
usually gone about performing their interpretive work.[7]

City Reading as "Misreading"

Forms might have helped to determine how city readers responded to their nineteenth-century environs, but this is not
to say the rituals of urban formalism were unburdened by
their share of difficulties.[8] There was always the risk that a
city reading (like any reading) depending on forms could
produce the kind of *mis*reading Michel de Certeau identified as a characteristic feature of an urban interpretive
practice that seemingly compelled city readers to choose
between wide-angled and pedestrian perspectives.[9] The city
as seen from the sidewalk, de Certeau reminds us, and the
city as seen from on high were never the same city. More
recently, Susan Wolfson has said that "'reading for form'
implies the activity as well as the object," as if to suggest
that forms were necessarily "enmeshed" in "historical conditions" in such an immediate way that any formalist practice
must itself possess all the vitality of a lived reality.[10] There is
nevertheless a record of a formalism that was much more
fraught than the one to which Wolfson, or even the more
ambivalent de Certeau, pays tribute. This mode of urban
formalism carried with it a core contradiction, the paradox
that sits at the center of this study. As expansive a practice as
urban formalism could be, it became an ironic one as well
when readers were induced to "miss" some aspect of the city
after becoming overly attentive to one form at the expense
of another.

    Most readers would have been more conversant in some

forms than they were in others, of course, but their proficiency was not invariably predicated upon their having an
affinity for this or that form. With that being said, we can
detect an interpretive pattern among the pattern makers, the
general population of urban formalists whom I've invoked
in opening this study. At any moment, it was possible for any
given formalist to become so preoccupied with forms that he
submitted to a kind of formal infatuation and so lost sight of
the city's other forms (or the idea that a city could be known
on something other than formal terms) as a result of his fixa-
tions. In focusing almost exclusively on any particular form,
a reader wasn't necessarily committing a *mis*reading, which
would imply there is a single "right" way to read. Rather,
the type of urban formalist who interests us simply took ob-
jectively questionable liberties with the freedoms that came
from having such a diversity of forms (and a diversity of ways
to read those forms) at her disposal. All of which is to say:
Readers were not above using and abusing forms, and there
were as many ways for a formalist reading of the city to occur
as there were readers, or as there were forms.

It's worth emphasizing that urban formalism had more
than negative potential. Even the unwitting reader, who
might not have been cognizant of his reliance on forms,
stood to benefit in his experiential grasp of the city from a
formally enhanced reception. Still, the very notion of urban apprehension continues to be regarded in some quar-
ters as a virtual impossibility. Hana Wirth-Neshner speaks
of "the problematic of reading cities," as if the making of
urban meaning could only result in some sort of impasse of
(mis)understanding.[11] My own account of this problem reck-
ons that readers have always read with such means as they
had at their disposal. The hazards that *all* city peoples ran in
performing any outwardly directed reading — from the prejudices they brought to bear on their own "situation" to the

interpretive conditions of a modern metropolis teeming with saturations, discontinuities, and distractions — were many.[12] Yet formalists confronted an additional difficulty in reading the city to the degree that they drew too close (in their highly personalized response, not their physical proximity) to its forms. "When no heed is paid to the relations that inhere in social facts," Henri Lefebvre has written, "knowledge misses its target."[13] That might serve as a fitting description of both the common causes and effects of the city readings we'll consider in what follows. We would be wrong to assume, however, that these readings (or their readers) failed in the act of urban interpretation simply because their interpretive methods and motivations differed from our own. Whatever these readers missed, they gained the comfort that their formal (dis)engagement with the city gave them. That in itself is worth inquiring into, and we will.

Chapter Outline

Urban Formalism is organized around four seminal examples of the kinds of forms to which formalists resorted, historically, when they were trying to make meaning from their cities. The first of these is the *textual* form of literature. The second is the *material* form of the big-city conflagration. The third is the *sociopolitical* form of revolutionary politics. And the fourth is the *visual* form of urban photography. If these are not the forms that my own readers might be expecting from a book such as this, they are just the forms to suggest how fluid was the range of interpretive registers in which urban formalists worked. A further word about the scope of my project is necessary. For the most part, I've drawn on formally invested city readings from what were arguably the leading metropolises in the transatlantic region during the nineteenth century, New York and Paris. There were, of course, important historical differences between these cities. But they were also, as Laure Katsaros explains, widely regarded as the "two celebrated faces of the modern city" on their respective continents.[14] As such they warrant the scrutiny I give to the unique brand of urban formalism they fostered.

As for the individual chapters of *Urban Formalism*, in Chapter 1 I explore a phenomenon that I call "Strong reading," by which I mean the act of reading urban life as if it were literature. Normally, we would identify both "Strong reading" and its close cousin, "misreading," with the Yale literary scholar Harold Bloom, for whom reading (and writing) is "a belated and all-but-impossible act" of struggle. Most of us, Bloom says, maintain a tenuous "relation to truth," since in our continuous "wrestling" with "texts" we lose sight of a "reality" that we tend to "treat as texts anyway."[15] The influential appeal of this theory notwithstanding, I find evidence in the historical record of a different kind of reading relation in the modern city. For at least one reader, there were certain advantages to accepting (rather than heroically resisting, as Bloom would have us do) a literary "relation to truth." For this particular reader, as for all readers, words were always going to position the world at a mediated distance. That's what words do. But for the Strong reader, the conventions that attended not only linguistic but self-consciously literary forms of mediation were less a force to be "wrestled" with than a welcome buffer against all kinds of untoward expressions of urbanism. We see this manner of city reading at work in the person and practices of a real nineteenth-century reader, George Templeton Strong, whose nominal reading practice was to treat entire cities as if they consisted of text and nothing but text.

I'm relying on Strong—a celebrated nineteenth-century lawyer, bibliophile, and diarist—to suggest the formal lengths to which a reader might go in trying to formulate a meaningful response to urban modernity's midcentury ascendance. Such was Strong's effusiveness as a formalist that it would be unfair to describe his interpretive habits as representative of city readers in the period. What's striking about those habits, what makes them worthy of our attention, are the outer limits they suggest for a formalism that's premised on an accentuated standard of literary discrimination. George Templeton Strong never did manage to assimilate his metropolis fully. Rather than relent in this effort, he turned his impressive stores of book learning onto the city, in the apparent belief that he could come to terms with New York by parsing his surroundings as if they comprised an actual literary text. By retreating to this interpretive posture in his confrontations with city scenes he couldn't comprehend, Strong passed the metropolis through a veritable looking glass of literature, as if Manhattan were a literal reflection of the kinds of poetic cadences, literary symbols, and word images he'd been conditioned by the generic language conventions of belles lettres to regard as normative. In this way he converted the city into a safer kind of formal (which is to say, verbal) spectacle. If Strong purchased this interpretive safe haven at the expense of a deeper appreciation for the multiplicity of peoples and untidy social processes that make and shape modernity, he did lay claim to a comforting—and, for us, instructive—reading strategy along the way.

In Chapter 2, we switch from a textual to a material examination of urban interpretation, to assess the kinds of formal responsiveness elicited by the nonverbal "object" of fire. We also move from attending to an elite reader such as George Templeton Strong to a more demotic population of fire "readers," some antebellum New York firemen among them. Under any conditions, urban formalism was rarely the insular quest for form that a city reader like Strong might have wished. His aesthetic expectations were frequently disappointed by the city's disordering realities, which left him susceptible to constant interpretive frictions brought on by the conflict between the metropolis that was and the metropolis he wanted. Fire readers also experienced interpretive frictions; these were no less meaningful because they differed in substance and reception strategy from Strong's literary formalism. Chapter 2 evaluates who fire readers were, how they came to read something seemingly unreadable, and why they insisted upon resorting to forms in dealing with a tragic fact of nineteenth-century life.

As an interpretive practice, there is something equivocal about fire reading. Contemporaries were so accustomed to seeing their cities laid to fiery waste that conflagration almost became synonymous for them with urban living. Archaic construction materials and methods, density of metropolitan development, and the delayed upgrade to a professional firefighting force meant that fires did not just burn in places like Manhattan. They burned often and arbitrarily, sometimes with devastating effects for city dwellers. Yet readers who longed for an interpretive sanctuary in the modern city were both frustrated and fascinated by fire's forms. On the one hand, cities burning brightly would evolve over the early middle decades of the century into a figure for urban disorder. Taking on a life of its own, fire thus became a universal sign for an entropic age. Not only was fire the scourge of a vulnerable urban infrastructure; it was a fitting emblem for a host of modern pathologies. Glaring socioeconomic inequalities, substandard living conditions among the urban poor, and mounting class antagonisms were just some of the more telling flashpoints of the metropolis in that day, as they remain in ours. When recast as a "form" for the firewatcher's decoding, the physically (not to mention financially) felt force of fire asserted itself as a more-than-metaphorical representation of a modernity beyond any one reader's control. On the other hand, for all the combustible trouble it did bring, fire retained the ability to delight the observer's eye as a "beautiful" thing. Considered from this perspective, the flickering light of fire was received by some readers less as an eruption of pent-up sociological menace than as a virtual museum piece designed to afford formal pleasure to anyone who needed psychic release from the daily pressures of metropolitan life. City readers had ample reasons to fear fire. Some of them were also prepared, rather perversely, to find something restorative in fire's form. We'll approach as near as we can to this perversity to examine fire-reading strategies in the then-reigning location of the city blaze, New York during the 1830s and after.

Rivaling fire for its range of unstable associations is France, which served the era's readers as yet another occasion for interpreting the urban. In Chapter 3, we consider how the divergent political experiences of the Paris métropole accumulated contrary meanings (a mixed reception, as it were) for interested onlookers during the tumultuous years of the nineteenth century. From the revolutionary close of the eighteenth century forward, modern France would undergo a century's worth of sociopolitical disturbance after the reign of Emperor Napoleon Bonaparte ended in 1814. The Franco-anarchic insurrection of the July Days from 1830, combined with the bloody socialist-inspired uprising of 1848 and the Paris Commune of 1871, was with justification a source of worry in the West. The Paris street protests led by radicalized segments of the working classes in 1848, especially, came to dominate journalistic headlines in both the United States and Europe for a time, such that one couldn't help but read about the daily battles being waged along the city's brick-lined killing grounds. Nor could watchers-on have desired a more majestic setting for contests that, beneath their tantalizing surface, were rooted in the endemic social problems that had made the City of Light as politically unstable as it was. As a "formal" event, partisan, populist upheaval garnered much attention; so, too, did the intensifying onset of an urbanization that was similarly giving modernity its shape in Europe. With the sensuous grandeur of Paris providing the platform for these developments as they played out in tandem — an urban revolution compounded by a political one — city readers could barely bring themselves to look away.

The meanings of these modern scenes were far from straightforward. Readers on the Continent, from Karl Marx to the expatriate American Margaret Fuller, may have been attuned to the unscripted *social* forms they associated with the radicalized working classes in France, whose future they regarded as an index of the evolution of modern industrial society. But these same readers were as equipped as any of their contemporaries to finesse the fine distinction (without a difference) that existed in Paris between the substance of a socially conscious politics and the "show" of its ideologically determined performance. In a city known for nurturing pleasure and that was looked to by many metropolitans worldwide as representing the beau ideal of civilized living, the staged refinements of the traditional arts and the spontaneous striving of social agitation bore too close a formal resemblance not to overlap. This was all the more the case for the nonparticipant in France's domestic drama, for whom city reading was often treated as a form of theater. Still, no matter how much the stereotypical forms of France, in the vacuum of abstraction, suggested elegance and entertainment, idleness and indulgence, a politics that was marked in Paris by rowdy manifestations of protoproletarian dissent was "real" in a way that artful aloofness might never be.

As a scene of urban response, the reactions to revolution

that were left on record in the Paris of 1848 afford us today, in
retrospect, a reception history of urban subversion as it was
registered in a cauldron of debate about the political orga-
nization of urban society. Some readers responded favorably
(whether in person or, for foreign observers, in absentia) to
a Paris of manufactured artistry and finery and so cast a figurative vote for lovely promenades and leisured heedlessness.
Some readers responded to the nation's recurrent occasions
of social disharmony with a sympathetic plea for comprehensive reform. A formalist response often sat somewhere
in between these readings, amid the volatile forms of urban
political unrest that attended this latest of France's repeated
revolutions. In trying to reconcile the conflicting meanings
of these forms, readers enlisted in as labored an undertaking
as they did in their interpretive encounters with fire or as
Strong did with his city addiction to literature.

The fourth and final mode of urban formalism that we
consider, in Chapter 4, is visual and took the form of urban photography. In the mechanical contrivance of the
daguerreotype, above all other variants of this technology,
many a "reader" discovered an attractive means of reworking
his impressions of the metropolis. The interpretive powers
that we attribute to a knowing, roving camera "eye" have
long engendered debates about the photographic medium:
whether its images relay a mimetic representation of the
"real" or a fabrication closer in kind to fiction. At the original time of their readings, readers further problematized
such questions by responding, as many of them did, to the
static images of a city that had been "frozen" by a fleeting
photographic moment. Such moments represented at best
a perceptual half-truth.

Because of its technical limitations and cumbersome requirements for prolonged exposure, the daguerreotype was
never a literal window onto the city. The photographic pro-

cess itself posed the by turns practical and philosophical paradox of whether and how a city that could not and would not
stand still might be interpreted by a mode of representation
that required its objects of observation to be stationary. This
new technology could offer up images of exquisite detail. It
could also produce composite pictures in which the pulsat-
ing life of the metropolis was more or less absent. In addressing this representational dilemma, I've compiled a selective
visual survey of some of the early city views from New York
and Paris that photography afforded the nineteenth-century
reader. The net effect of this archival evidence is revealing.
Assisted by an invention that was supposed to help readers
"see," city readers were left to redress the perpetual, if productive, imbalance of their encounters with images that
were as faithful to the representation of social facts as they
were implicated in the overdetermined display of the most
chillingly "artistic" of forms. The form of the urban photograph is a visual extension of a modernity that, given the period's proliferation of observational options, had succeeded
in opening up the most unlikely possibilities for perception.

At the foundational stage of nineteenth-century urbanism, readers had their pick of which forms they'd use to
navigate their way around the city. Urban contexts under
these conditions might become literary texts. Ordinary objects could metamorphose into extraordinary artifacts. Im-
provisational politics were sometimes narrowly regarded as
nonevents. And visual images were candidates for becoming
pictures of a metropolis recomposed by human machinery.
None of these means of receiving a new urban world was inevitable. Each was the quiet byproduct of a vacillating urge
to shift the interpretative basis of being — of being modern,
that is — back and forth between studious engagement and
artful rearrangement, modes of perception that were by no
means mutually exclusive. This urge in turn complicated

the city respondent's absorption in what and how he was reading. From this perceptual point forward, certain kinds of readers (urban formalists, historically understood) made an understated show of taking in, on their own terms, the beguiling variety of life that had taken shape around them. It could be said they missed much as a result. It's more likely the case that, given their early proficiency in the handling of forms, these readers set an important precedent for a robust and multidimensional brand of urban interpretation that remains with us to this day.

1

Strong Reading, or the Literary Conversion of the Urban

What set our bourgeois apart from others . . . was his obsession with completeness. He wanted to capture his entire city, every bit of it.
— ROBERT DARNTON, *The Great Cat Massacre*

For the twenty-year-old New York law clerk George Templeton Strong, the most objectionable thing in any piece of printed literature was what he called "wildness," whether of style, content, or form. This, at least, was the position he took on April 6, 1840, while writing in the leather-bound collection of oversized copybooks that Strong liked to call his private journal, or diary.[1] Strong's outlook on cities was little different than his tastes in literature. He expected to be able to read the one precisely as he read the other: at his own leisure, and with the calm assurance that his regular passage through his native Manhattan would be as safe and smooth and pleasing to the senses as any gratifying encounter with a good book. Strong was hardly unaware of what was happening, in his own words, in "the streets of New York" (*DGTS* I,

11: March 7, 1836). Indeed, what he described as the "state of things out of doors" was seldom far from his mind (I, 55–56: April 7, 1837). But as "a modern reader" (that's his phrase), he insisted on having his literary and urban sensibilities align perfectly, as if the city were a traditional "text" to be read like any other (I, 11: March 7, 1836).

As an urban formalist, Strong was the consummate literalist. He approached the work of urban interpretation by imposing his preference for formal coherence upon a city that, given its dynamic and changeable qualities, resisted any such practice. What recommends Strong to our attention is not the presumption of his impositions. Rather, he provides a conspicuous historical instance of a formalism that has severed its connection with the lived experience of the city, an experience with which we are still coming to terms today. In his account of what he names "urban palimpsests," Andreas Huyssen speaks of the "memory fatigue" that city readers can endure when they peel back the continuously added layers of urban lives that have already been *lived*. Huyssen writes that the "form" of this "mise-en-scène of modernity," composed of everything from monuments and museums to a city's general public spaces, is "without borders" and has made the urban past unnervingly present in a way that we might assume would be anathema to someone of a conservative temperament like Strong's.[2] Yet Strong was unsettled far more by the form of the urban present than he was by that of the past. His example serves to remind us of the problematic consequences that can ensue when a reader tries to make the forms that are all around him, at any given moment, fit his preconceived notions of what a city (or a literature) should be.

At the same time, there is a favorable word to be said for the impulse to stake one's understanding of the city's dizzying complexity on what the historians Edwin Burrows and

Mike Wallace call the "patterns we discern amid the swirl of events." Much as the authors of *Gotham: A History of New York to 1898* (1998) have attempted, in their own telling, to "present a picture of urban life as a rounded whole," George Templeton Strong took such steps as he deemed necessary to render his city decipherable.[3] This was the case despite the noticeable exaggerations of Strong's interpretive practice. He might have made formal compromises, but the distinctive version of urban formalism he practiced was not wholly compromised. We're led back to his example as much for what he gained from formalism, perceptually speaking, as for what he lost because of his deep-seated need for the organic forms of his city — its peoples, places, pastimes, and, yes, its patterns — to match his impossible standards of virtuous uniformity.

If Strong's reading practice was unique, it does invite comparison with the urban interpretive methods of his contemporaries. Among the most recognizable of these was a type of city reading that I'd call *disambiguation*. Its practitioners constituted a class of readers, joined as many (but not all) of them were by status aspirations and consolidating market forces that set them at a critical distance from the workaday world.[4] These readers came to the work of city reading through a sense of unwanted obligation; the transformative economies, societies, and infrastructures of cities suggested to them a troubled text that demanded close inspection. Modern cities were for these readers one of "the great signifying structures of the age," John Kasson explains, "vast, intricate repositories" at once "dense with meaning" in their untold variety yet potentially "unintelligible in terms of any earlier coherent system of signs." How to unravel what Kasson describes as an unwieldy urban scene of "compressed, tangled, contrasting, chaotic, and often opaque surfaces" was not just a "challenge to interpretation," as Hans

Bergmann contends. It was a dangerous straddling of the
line between seeming "chaos and meaninglessness," on the
one hand, and, on the other, a normalizing drive to restore
what Michel Foucault has called the "order of things."[5]

This ambivalence about cities was a characteristic feature of the disambiguating mode of city reading. In his self-
negating survey of "humanity in the city," for example, the
New York pastor Edwin Hubbel Chapin commemorates the
"multitudinous" city streets of 1854 as "something finer than
the grandest poetry," only to betray the instability of his own
metaphor by substituting in quick, hesitant succession the
alternative analogies of "an inspiring lyric" and "an epic,
rather" for the city's "sweeping," "inexhaustible procession"
of "the contrasts, the conflicts, the heroisms, and failures . . .
of human life." Visiting Cincinnati at midcentury, the German journalist and travel writer Moritz Busch was prepared,
for his part, to compare the nation's then-sixth-largest urban settlement "to a great newspaper page," inasmuch as
"the yard-long columns of journals" could be said to "cor-
respond" to "the mile-long streets of the city." This is not to
say that Busch's city was readable; it was an "illustration,"
instead, of what he called "superabundant confusion." New
York's native son Isaac Lyon would have agreed. The up-
wardly mobile "catch" cartman Lyon considered himself a
veritable "encyclopedia" of Manhattan after spending several decades there canvassing the island's "many mazy and
intricate windings." It was, in his estimation, this "labor . . .
of a lifetime" that had allowed him to "learn his A, B, C's"
and so attain through a long tenure in urban "investigation"
the "intelligence" needed to be something other than func-
tionally illiterate, "like a blind man groping his way in the
dark."[6] Any city reading that was construed in this way entailed a reaction to a text that, if it couldn't be tamed, was
to be interpreted according to the terms normally reserved

for an essentially stabilizing encounter with language and literature.[7]

There were, of course, a range of available ways to read the city, among them a Strong reading, which I've only begun to describe. Close in kind to disambiguation, Strong reading also aims at a harmonious combination of formal and social order in its anxious drive to master an unmanageable metropolitan text. If they tend toward a similar end, however, these two modes of reading nevertheless distinguish themselves by their divergent means. Disambiguation feels like *work*. That is to say, it carries with it the weighted responsibility of having to make those aspects of the city that have proved most resistant to interpretation more meaningfully transparent. Strong's reading, by contrast, was less a form of work than interpretive play, by which he set about securing the pleasure of registering the city's most appealing (to him, at any rate) aesthetic effects through his love of literature. The one reader labors his way toward urban order. The other strives at making the city more intelligible by *not* straining. Both aimed at gaining what Carl Smith calls "imaginative control over the city."[8]

Other readers shared Strong's preference for seamless text over messy context without adopting his exact practice. In the initial prefatory statement from 1840 for their ambitious literary journal *Arcturus*, New Yorkers Evert Duyckinck and Cornelius Mathews pronounced "Books" a "refuge from the material daily occupations for self which more or less employ every one." Many more readers held to this sentiment, to judge from those who recorded the joys they experienced in occupying themselves solely with literature. A writer for the March 1844 issue of the *Expositor and Universalist Review* praised poetry, in particular, for its ability to "carry the mind beyond and above the beaten, dusty, weary walks of ordinary life." The author Leroi Lee meanwhile maintained that such reading required but "the smallest part" of "labour" and promised in return maximum "leisure" for anyone who "possessed, in a remarkable degree, the power of abstracting his mind from surrounding objects." Even our industrious cartman Isaac Lyon would concede the attractiveness of an interpretive position that situated him above the fray of his everyday concerns. Hard at work from dawn to dusk, he writes of having "spent many hundreds of my evenings in the different book auction rooms" of Manhattan, where he "always" took "some satisfaction in seeing and handling a rare and valuable book, and hearing its secret history descanted upon, even if [he were] not able to become the owner of it." And with "the general book-trade," as the newspaperman Asa Greene avers, thriving across the country, both "within doors" and "without," the period's readers perhaps naturally succumbed to what Lyon again calls "bibliomania on the brain to a greater or less extent." Strong not only made reading a "necessity of life," as the historian William Gilmore says of early nationals in the United States generally. He and the readers who shared his sensibilities assumed that life and literature were interchangeable, with the one both reflecting and informing the other.[9]

By the Book

Before George Templeton Strong ever came to conflate city reading with literary reading—he once compared the "muddy" lyrics of the English Romantic poet Percy Bysshe Shelley to "a puddle in the middle of the road," much as he had earlier complained that an unusually rainy March had left the streets of New York "thickened with mud to the consistence of molasses"—he made as thoroughgoing a study of Manhattan as he had of the various libraries and booksellers in his vicinity (*DGTS* I, 42: November 28, 1836; I, 11–12:

March 7, 1836). Strong effectively slipped into the ebb and flow of urban surroundings that were very much in flux as he approached adulthood in the 1830s. New York's exponential growth in the period matched Strong's own march to maturity; he and his Manhattan came of age together. What had been a promising northern port city of 33,000 residents in 1790 was by 1850 the U.S. capital of banking, trade, and finance, with a local population of upward of half a million people. By 1861, that number stood at 800,000, making New York the largest urban center not only in the United States but the entire Western Hemisphere. New York as it emerged in this midcentury phase was a genuine modern metropolis. In its diversity, economy, and increasingly unstable society, it resembled the kind of "inchoate" environments of "explosive conflicts and jarring discontinuities" that David Henkin has characterized as "reliable metonyms" of civic disorder, public anomie, and private quandary.[10] This was George Templeton Strong's master text, which he read with unfeigned frustration. There's no question that Strong held an abiding affection for his birthplace. A "very great city is this," he writes, "with all its absurdities" (I, 305: October 29, 1847). He was also cognizant of what he laments are the "drawbacks of a city," which figured for him a powerful "force of contrast" with New York's charms, such as they were (I, 23: June 9, 1836; I, 145: August 1, 1840).

The process of Strong's coming into urban consciousness was no more systematic than his initiation — as an avid reader, finder, and buyer of books — into an inimitable New York world of print. We simply cannot understand how Strong read his city unless we account for the practical matter of where and when and what he was reading. Maternally educated at home in his formative years, Strong was already reading at the tender age of four.[11] By the fall of 1832, a twelve-year-old Strong was studying at Columbia's grammar school, where he excelled in his courses in Greek and Latin. But when he wasn't keeping up with his coursework, Strong was reading "miscellaneously" (*DGTS* I, 161: May 25, 1841; I, 187: September 30, 1842). That's how he later portrayed his habit of foraging for books that extended well beyond his assigned studies. To this end Strong made frequent "rambles," as he calls them, about town in pursuit of the choicest reading materials he could locate (I, 53: March 25, 1837; I, 101: April 10, 1839). These urban excursions amounted to an intensive tutorial in city reading. Ever restless to obtain more to read, Strong enlisted in an urban learning process premised on what became his *a priori* relation to literary texts.[12]

His ranging back and forth across New York for books was in some respects a preliminary step to his seasoned response, as a reader, to his city. Strong speaks of a "general run on books" in these years and advises that it "is as well to secure . . . books . . . whenever they can be found" (*DGTS* I, 106: June 3, 1839). Auctions were one place where he looked, despite the inflated prices arising from the public's "eagerness to buy" (I, 100: March 15, 1839).[13] Libraries afforded another option. There was the collection at Columbia College, where he matriculated in 1834; it was open to students, faculty, and alumnae on Saturdays from noon to 3 pm, "as the statutes allow" (I, 3: October 10, 1835). There was the law library at his father's Wall Street office, too, where, at the start of his three-year clerkship in October 1838 — and continuing thereafter for an additional three years of legal reading — Strong obtained the "law calves" that he needed to prepare for the bar exam (I, 96: December 19, 1836). There were also sizeable holdings at the New York Society Library, on Chambers Street. With his father's backing in March 1838, Strong purchased the share of a retiring subscription member and so enjoyed access to an array of books and periodicals he otherwise would have had to scramble to find.

Strong liked to buy before he borrowed, and he haunted
the city's bookstores in tireless pursuit of texts, even before he
commanded his own income as a partner at his law firm. It
was a labor of love, with much legwork and accustomed confusion. In a city as big as Manhattan, there was no telling the
outcome of one's purchasing expeditions. Some of Strong's
ended in disappointment. A regular patron of Appleton's, on
Broadway, he applauded the day in November 1836 when
the proprietor "expanded so that the Old Books, instead of
being literally crammed upstairs"—such that "it was scarcely
possible to navigate . . . for the folios that were heaped up in
piles six or eight feet high"—"will be provided with some sort
of decent accommodation below" (*DGTS* I, 41: November 3,
1836). Yet having "looked into" this same retailer's "new assortment of old books" one afternoon three years on, Strong
still regrets to say that his mainstay supplier has only "a gi-
gantic basket full" of "sad trash" on this occasion, a dismissal
that could as readily apply to the storefront outside as the
inventory within (I, 107: June 19, 1839). When desirable reading was "not to be had there," Strong "hunted about a good
while" in hope of "catching a copy" that struck his fancy
elsewhere (I, 49: January 7, 1837). These trips more often
than not met with greater success. Strong frequently stopped
by Bancroft's bookstore, Gurley's, and Wiley & Putnam's
establishments as well, and "as a last resort went into that ras-
cally citadel of humbug, Colman's" (I, 49: January 7, 1837).

Strong spared no expense in his acquisitions. At times
he admonished that "economy must be my rule of life for a
little while"—this, after having "laid out eight dollars of my
capital on Ben Jonson, with which investment I am well
pleased" (*DGTS* I, 102: April 23, 1839). Yet a "great work"
like James Audubon's illustrated *The Birds of America* (1840)
exceeded the resources of even this inveterate collector. "It's
a fine book," Strong decides, after viewing the volume at

Columbia in January 1842. "I wish I could afford to own
a copy" (I, 174: January 10, 1842).[14] But whether flush with
funds or not, this reader insisted on quality inside and out,
what he calls "point of show." So, when Strong happened
upon "the finest possible condition as to binding and typog-
raphy" — "the best and richest kind" was most to his liking —
he was willing to pay "additional" for the privilege of owning
a text that could be set out on display (I, 55: April 7, 1837;
I, 69–70: June 20, 1837). This is not to say that Strong scorned
cheap print. He mentions the "penny press" by name, along
with the "glorious trio" of high-circulation newspaper titles
("the *Sun*, *Transcript*, and *Herald*") that we would not normally associate with a man of his social standing (I, 190: November 17, 1842; I, 24: June 11, 1836). Strong was, in other
words, prepared to look high and low for his literatures
throughout the city, much as he was ready to spend whatever
he needed to spend.

Both contemporary accounts and the literary estate catalog published in 1878, three years after Strong's death, open
up a world of words unlike any other reader's from the era.[15]
In his *Private Libraries of New York*, the physician James
Wynne celebrates the "labors" of collectors like Strong,
whose "miscellaneous" assortment ("strongest," he says, "in
History, and in English and German literature") of some
four to five thousand books and manuscripts he ranks among
the two dozen or so most notable in midcentury Manhattan.[16] Of these, 1,763 selections would be sold by Strong's
surviving family at auction in November 1878. Strong ex-
pended a small fortune in compiling his collection, while
he canvassed a city that was also very much in the making.
An alphabetical sampling suggests how immense a work
Strong's reading was (Table 1).

Strong organized his collection while compiling it; he
did the same for his city. For in seeking far and wide for his

Table 1. Strong Reading, from the Strong Library. Estate Catalog Selections, 1878.

	Author	Title	Publication	Condition
A	N/A	Architecture. A Glossary of Terms, used in Grecian, Roman, and Gothic . . .	Oxford, Parker, 1845 4th ed.	Exemplified by Eleven Hundred Wood-Cuts. Vol. 1, Text. Vol. 2, Plates. 2 vols, 8 vo, full calf
B	Ballantine, James	Treatise on Painted Glass	Edinburgh, 1845	Numerous colored illustrations. 8 vo, half russia
C	Cuvier, Baron	The Animal Kingdom, Arranged in Conformity with its Organization	London, 1827–1832	Numerous Illustrations. 15 vols. and Index. Together 16 vols, tree calf, gilt edges
D	Didbin, Rev. Thomas F.	The Library Companion; or, the Young Man's Guide and the Old Man's Comfort in the Choice of a Library	London, 1825 2nd ed.	8 vo, full russia
E	N/A	ΕΚΣΚΥΒΑΛΑΥΡΟΝ; or, The Discovery of a most exquisite Jewel . . .	London, 1652	Curious Portrait. 32 mo. full calf
F	Feuillet, Octave.	Scènes et Comedies	Paris, 1854	12 mo, half morocco
G	Goethe, Johann.	Faust; Part II. Translated partly in the Metres of the Original, and partly in Prose, with other Poems, by Leopold J. Bernays	London, 1839	8 vo, calf
H	Hakluyt, Richard	The Principal Navigations . . .	Imprinted at London by George Bishop, 1599–1600	A Beautiful copy of the genuine edition
I	N/A	Illustrated London News, with all the Supplements	London, 1842–1856	Vols. 1 to 28 inclusive, bound in 19, folio, half morocco
J	Johnson, Samuel	A Dictionary of the English Language . . .	London, 1825	Portrait. 2 vols, 4to, half russia

Table 1. (continued).

	Author	Title	Publication	Condition
K	Kant, Immanuel	*Critick of Pure Reason. Translated from the Original . . .*	London, Pickering, 1838	8 vo, cloth
L	Lesage, Alain-René	*The Adventures of Gil Blas of Santillane. Translated from the French by T. Smollett.*	London, 1836	Illustrated by Jean Gioux. 2 vols., royal 8 vo, half morocco
M	Machiavel, Nicholas	*The Art of Warre. Written in Italian by Nicholas Machiavel, and set forth in English by Peter Withorne, Student at Graies Inn.*	Imprinted at London by Thomas East, for John Wright, 1588	Maps, Drawings of Fortifications, &c. Very Scarce.
N	N/A	*Natural History of New York:* Agriculture, 5 vols.; Botany, 2 vols.; Geology, 4 vols.; Mineralogy, 1 vol.; Palæontology, 2 vols.; Zoology, 5 vols.	New York, 1843	Profusely Illustrated with all the beautiful Engravings, many of which are richly colored. 19 vols., 4to, half Russia, gilt top
O	N/A	*Oxonia Illustrata. Sive Omnium Celeberrimae istius Universitatis Collegiorum Aularum Bibliothecae Bodleianae Scholarum Publicarum . . .*	Oxoniae, 1675	40 Double Engravings. Folio, calf
P	Petrarca, Francesco	*Secretum seu De Contemptu Mundi . . .*	Leiner de Reutlingen, 1473	Bound together in 1 vol, folio, full morocco. Very fine copies
Q	N/A	*The Quarterly Review*	London, 1809–1850	Including 4 index vols. 87 vols., 8 vo, half calf

R	N/A	*Royal Gems from the Galleries of Europe. Engraved after the Pictures of the Great Masters . . .*	London (n.d.)	With Notices, Biographical, Historical, and Descriptive, by S. C. Hall. Steel Engravings. Folio, half morocco, cloth sides. Fine impressions of the plates
S	Spenser, Edmund	*The Shepheard's Calender*	London, Printed by Thomas Creede, for John Harrison the yonger, 1597	4 to, full morocco, gilt edges. Black Letter. A Very Scarce Edition
T	Tennyson, Alfred	*Works*	London, 1872	Fine Library Edition. With Portrait. 6 vols., 8 vo, half morocco, gilt top
U	Uhland, L.	*Volkslieder*	Stuttgart, 1844	2 vols., 8 vo, half morocco
V	Virgillii	*Opera Omnia*	Argentorati, Johann Cruninger, M.D. II	With Numerous Illustrations. Very rare edition; with many exceedingly curious woodcuts
W	Wordsworth, William	*The Poems of*	London, 1845	Portrait and Frontispiece. 8vo, full morocco, gilt edges
X	Xenophontis	*Francisci Philelfi Praefatio in Xenophontis Libros de Cyripaedia ad Paulum Secundum Pontificem Maximum*	s.l., 1467	Fine Copy. Very Scarce. Wide margin. 4to, old calf
Y	Young, Edward	*The Poetical Works of*	London, 1844	Portrait. Pickering Edition. 2 vols, 16 mo, full morocco, gilt edges
Z	Ziemann, A.	*Mittelhochdeutsches Wörterburg, nebst Grammatischer Einleitung*	Leipzig, 1838	8 vo, half russia

reading, Strong traveled the coordinates of a cognitive map,
lavishly illustrated and bound in finely tooled leather. Cu-
vier's natural taxonomies, Samuel Johnson's ambitious lexicon, and Hakluyt's seafaring navigations, to mention a few of
the books at his disposal, all indicate a mind and a man like
Isaac Lyon, undertaking to "learn his A, B, C's" by reading
and mentally sorting his city in tandem.[17] Strong surveyed
a fair amount of Manhattan and came away from his observations with the mixed response of a not-quite-converted
urban dweller who was disappointed to find a less than
general prevalence of agreeable aesthetic effects. A Sunday
stroll from October 1840 is typical in this respect. Walking
"up to Eighth Street and down again," Strong concludes,
"It's a pity we've no street but Broadway that's fit to walk in
of an evening. The street is always crowded, and whores and
blackguards make up about two-thirds of the throng." There
was a remedy at hand, however. Strong believes that "one
of the advantages of uptown" (Strong at this time was still
living at his parents' well-appointed townhouse, downtown)
was that "the streets there are well paved, well lighted, and
decently populated" (DGTS I, 150: October 11, 1840). Much
like a library, a city could be set straight, provided certain
notions of decorum prevailed.

Strong meanwhile took control of his immediate affairs.
"Stayed at home all the morning putting my library in order"
is how he articulates a recurring theme of his days, and of his
diary (DGTS I, 14: March 30, 1836). Indeed, "arranging my
books" qualifies for Strong as more than a description of his
stay-at-home labors; it articulates his highest interpretive de-
sires, codified in the maxim that his library would "require
an overhauling about twice a year" (I, 53: March 24, 1837).
Strong was alive to his eccentric side, epitomized by an almost manic anxiety to keep tabs on his texts. But keeping a
close watch on his literary possessions was serious business

for Strong. The ordering work that occurred in his library was an indirect manifestation of the genuine hardships that he confesses attended his efforts at reading. "But the fact is I'm yet a novice in the art of reading," he admits. "I have got myself into a sad habit of careless, desultory, hasty reading, running over the words but not the ideas, and I must break myself of it" (I, 70: June 22, 1837). Having "suffered" himself "to get into" an "infamous habit of careless slip slop reading," Strong took care to rectify tendencies that threatened to disrupt his sense of himself as a reader of words in a modern world (I, 93: October 29, 1838).

Some Strong Readings

Seeing Strong read Henry Wadsworth Longfellow's poem "The Beleaguered City" gives us a closer view of his reading practice in action. Strong's reception of Longfellow was of course preconditioned. He had fairly fixed notions of prosody by the time he graduated from Columbia in 1838, and he became familiar with the New England writer's work in the wake of his burgeoning reputation. Strong read the "great man's" prose romance *Hyperion* in the summer of 1839, "and it led me to think highly," he records, "of his taste and abilities, though there's some smoke in it." It was Longfellow's urban verse that most struck him. This "little poem of his," which Strong saw in the *Southern Literary Messenger* in November 1839, is "great," he says, paying Longfellow the further Coleridgean compliment of rating the work in question as "worthy of the author of *The Ancient Mariner*" (*DGTS* I, 113–14: November 12, 1839).[18]

Longfellow begins his poem at the point where Strong receives it. The introductory stanza opens with an inscribed reader, reading: "I have read of some old, wondrous tale, / Some legend strange and vague, / That a midnight host of spectres pale / Beleaguer'd the walls of Prague." This is the setting where we receive Longfellow's retelling of the urban "legend" of a city under siege. Our first impressions are of a mirror-like reflection of another reader, with whose likeness we are implicitly asked to identify from the outset. Temporally removed from today — the speaker has drawn on "some old, wondrous tale," he informs us — the "strange" city of Prague that appears in this passage is spatially inaccessible, too, since American readers arrive at the scene of this shadowy "midnight" image only after imaginatively crossing an ocean, a continent, and, we learn in the next stanza, "the Moldau's rushing stream," this last an archaic invocation of the Czech Vltava River. Because readers have reached this chimera of a city "as in an awful dream," it poses no more threat to us than it does the unnamed peoples of the poem's legendary setting. The threat is merely metaphorical; it inheres in the spiritual figure of the "ghastly" fears that rush upon all of us in the "sorrowful" hours of night/life, but it can be dispelled by a dawning "glorious morning" of "prayer" that's heralded in the timeless ringing of some "old cathedral bell."

What Strong considers most "Glorious" in Longfellow's text, echoing in his excitement the poet's very diction of resplendence, is the "beautiful and forcible comparison" on which it turns to achieve meaning (*DGTS* I, 113–14: November 12, 1839). The poem's initial six quatrains refer to a decidedly poetic Prague. Its latter half represents another mirrored image: in this iteration, of our same first-person reader, still reading, but from an ostensibly different text on which we receive an additional six quatrains of figurative description. Even less "real" than before, the city evoked in these latter passages is metaphysical, in that it operates primarily at the level of fabulous analogy. "I have read in the wondrous heart of man," the speaker intones, "That

strange and mystic scroll, / That an army of phantoms, vast
and wan, / Beleaguer the human soul." Now the site of interpretive contact has shifted to a "wondrous" work; this is
the "human" condition itself, hypothetically rendered. As
before, "The spectral camp is seen." Again it is the chiming
"deep church bell," commemorating in conventional tones
the hour of prayer, which breaks the "spell" of "ghastly fear."
Once more we watch as "The shadows sweep away" before
the walls of a sturdy urban fortress, which remains standing
unshaken. In the end, the "midnight battleground" setting
the scene in both the poem's diptych halves is a familiar one
to the extent that it's a *formal* one. And that is what Strong
wanted in his reading, the formal assurance that our lives
could be as lyrically composed (in the multiple meanings of
that word) as our literatures. As Strong would write in 1852,
"There is poetry enough latent in the South Street merchant
and the Wall Street financier; . . . in the omnibus driver that
conveys them all from the day's work to the night's relax-
ation and repose; in the brutified denizens of the Points and
the Hook; . . . and in the future of each and all" (II, 201–11:
July 5, 1852).[19]

If no one else performed the work of urban interpretation
in quite the same way as Strong, others demonstrated an
equally instrumental affinity for urban formalism in these
years. One such reader was the New York butcher Thomas
Farrington De Voe. Like Strong, the successful businessman
De Voe (by 1840, he was representing his fellow butchers
during trade negotiations with the city, and by 1872 he'd
been appointed to the position of superintendent of markets) held firm convictions on the proper form a city should
take. Also in sympathy with Strong, he took steps to formally
recompose his personal conception of Manhattan in accordance with the methodical, stabilizing march of his own career. Indeed, throughout the measured course of his climb

to middle-class prosperity, De Voe made sure to read the
straight and narrow course of his life back into the surrounding city, such that the predictably rigid and regular patterns
by which he imagined his metropolis must have qualified for
him as a kind of psychic necessity.

As a respected antiquarian and book collector,[20] and as a
writer who composed a full-length history of his city's markets, a volume De Voe saw published in 1862 as *The Market
Book,* he was a fully engaged city reader. And he was, like
Strong, an urban formalist of "literary" proportions. In the
quiet household solitude of his study, De Voe maintained
an exhaustive record of what and how he was reading. Compiled today as his *Historical Incidents from Newspapers,* De
Voe's *Incidents* is for all intents and purposes the most skele-
tal of commonplace books. *Incidents* reads as an understated
itemization of all the reported facts from the daily news that
our citizen butcher thought were worth preserving in his
mediated encounters with the "text" of the city. Reflexive
but not penetrative, brisk but without building any kind of
comprehensive storyline or forward narrative momentum,
De Voe's minimalist account of the mornings and evenings
he spent poring over the city's published journals is *de-
votional* in name only. He had, after all, merely skimmed
the surface of a world and worldview composed wholly of
the fixed-width columns of newsprint. De Voe can be said to
have exceeded the restrictive limits he set himself in at least
one respect, since he surveyed a full panoply of mostly New
York newspapers. Still, he appears to have been uninterested
in varying his interpretive surveys by genre. He chose for
the most part to ignore the alternative print venues of books,
magazines, and annuals. In contrast to other city readers,
De Voe furthermore seems to have been warily aware, despite his abiding curiosity, of the startling variety of cultural
forms on offer in his city, that kaleidoscope of images which

commentators from Baudelaire to Walter Benjamin have highlighted in their respective studies of the "readable" signs of urban modernity.[21] The laconic, self-effacing phrases contained in De Voe's periodic entries for this reason read more as the cross-ruled lines from an actuarial ledger than they resemble the conventionally expatiating space of a personal journal. As we can see in Figure 1.1, De Voe's shorthand scan of the city's *Commercial Advertiser* (his newspaper of choice) for 1835 suggests a fertile if not an inquiring mind. We receive hints here of a cognition that was as satisfied with the clipped offerings of an informational dispatch as it was with anything that might fall under the heading of the sensational, the spectacular, or the dramatic. On the evidence of his *Incidents*, De Voe did not want anything that even remotely approached the qualities of drama. He wanted not effusion but concision, not a spectacle but the reassuring containment of that most easily apprehensible of forms, the unadorned list. His *Incidents* reads as one man's internal map of Manhattan's rectilinear grid, that famous official layout of the island which was codified in 1811 by the Commissioner's Plan for New York City (Figure 1.2).

By singling out certain items for mention in his *Incidents*, De Voe signals their being significant; by reducing this significance to a chronological assemblage of bare facts, he reveals the less-is-more priorities of a reader willing to sacrifice the unruliness of "ordinary" forms to his individuated vision of a city that could be tidily aligned within the neat confines of a notebook page. De Voe's entry in *Incidents* for April 19 duly makes terse mention of a "Riot at Baltimore." September 7 brings less than revolutionary news from Paris, there being an "attempt" on the Continent upon the life of "Phillipe. Louis. King of France." Then comes a succession of days that sets down a string of prosaic developments at home. Their ordinariness is precisely the formal pattern they

1835. The Commercial &c continued

Aug. 17 Davis, Jefferson resigns for lieut. of Gov., sons.
17 Riot in Baltimore.
" Tiger. Loose near Harlaem. Bulldogs & hunting the 21 that suffered for
20 Hound that Joiners adopted.
24 Braces measure. Aug. 2.32 to shot.
26 Ambition. rushings against. 28. Sept. 12. 16.
29 Moon: Great Glory about discoveries in this   Locke's
" City. Its sale for an hospital, carriages & Holland. St. Croix organ. Paris evidence.
31 Military. Mech. Gray Capt. Leonard Compy. see Nov 24, when
Sept. 2 Poughkeepsie. Shooting. 2d. 3d. 4.th 3.
3 Stolen property. 23 st. 7 av. in bole sides.
" Land. Issued. 12 Clinton, published a notice of his leaving his wife.
" Ulster County. 2 st. No. 4. dwelling.
4 Tappan. Arthur. reward offered for him. South. 5.
7 Phillipe. Louis. King of France attempt upon his life. Wend.th 9.
10 Wooden block pavement put down in Broadway, foot 23. Nov. 13.
12 Steamboat rising in the world and North America.
17 Stamford. Post St. marine of foot to michael. Dog faults in Blue Houses.
" Nibler's Garden. Fire at. with pictures. st. work
19 Fleschie's Infernal Machine.
Oct. 1 Hoit's Hotel 2 ad for 175.000 dollars
5 Hail. Road. Tunnell Hos. views.
6 Nobles characters in a space. handed off and in pinnacle.
7 Mechanics Fair at Castle Garden.
12 Barnegat Pirate. Trial of the
13 Hudson. Sabbath. historical ramblings.
" Wall Street Swindler of 41 as a broker. Young Dandy
15 Distance. Harrington 1. with pictures of Flying van
17 Omnibus. Broadway. Columbus and Scholastic. Oct 12. 29
27 American Institute. Toasts to Col. Knapp. June.
" Foreman's Guide by districts.
28 Mansion House. James F. De Peyster's burnt down. see Alban'n Day time
29 New York City buildings. evening. 2 page. see on Nov 3
" Theatre. Thompson's letter on Women of the town. Beecher's
Nov. 2 Ferry. Fulton and South. lease. Oct. 29.
" Balloon. Wise. Nov 6. June 6. wise.
10 Underbrook. Heavy f of and. Packard by Knockaway (in Compy.)
25 Steamboats. First by Fitch.
Dec. 8 Webster. Dan'l. Large Scenes presented to   (see Jan'y 4 1836)
14 Bear killed. Large in Vermont 439 lb.
17 Five. Great millions of, of effect. 16. 17. dispn. 21. 22.
19 Wilkins. Louis. heroism in saving a child (Child) reward &c, the President

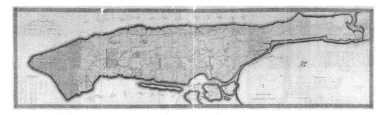

Figure 1.2. Map of the city of New York and island of Manhattan, as laid out by the commissioners appointed by the legislature, April 3, 1807. Collection of the Library of Congress.

inscribe for the writer. On September 10, there is word of "wooden block pavement put down in Broadway." October 7 records a "Mechanics Fair at Castle Garden." The 29th of that same month notes a "New York City building erecting." His list runs on and on, as De Voe proceeds to document in his signature telegrammatic style a metropolitan infrastructure of things but not thoughts. De Voe's world is one of omnibuses, steamboats, railroads, and ferries. He lives, breathes, and reads real estate transactions, municipal elections, court hearings, art institute openings, diorama exhibits, and tinkers with their "machines."[22] This is not to suggest that De Voe entirely lacks the sensitive range of perspectives we would associate with the complexity of subjectivity. It is to say he's a reader who favors an odd combination of inclusiveness (a quality we encounter with many urban formalists), reductiveness (a quality De Voe associates with formal economy), and recursiveness (a quality the rest of us associate with formal redundancy). Whatever forms there were to be discovered in his city — and there were an abundance of them, as the remarkable range of his entries makes clear — De Voe gave them a strict and controlling sense of shape by slotting them inside the tightest-fitting formal structure he

could find. This was not at all a question of his indifference
to the city's plurality of forms; it was a question of his resorting to a particular type of form to achieve the sort of interpretive reassurance he required. There was drama enough in
De Voe's being able to rearrange the remains of the day, inside his *Incidents*, from something exciting and exceptional
into something "incidental." However we might feel about
De Voe's squeezing Manhattan inside a form-fitting table,
we must admit that he'd located a form that satisfied his own
expectations of what a city should be.

The Urban World of Work

As did De Voe, Strong formalized his response to modernity
at a pivotal moment in the history of American class relations in the northeastern cities of the United States. Strong
was on hand to observe a new set of class formations take
shape as a result of the profound changes in labor practices
in the period, changes that had largely eroded the autonomy
of the urban working classes. Several factors contributed to
this diminishment of urban workers' comparative independence. To begin, the protoindustrialization that occurred
during the first half of the nineteenth century reorganized
work in its essentials, introducing increased measures of
mechanization while depersonalizing the relations between
employers and employees. This trend toward specialized
and subdivided wage labor precipitated a related decline in
the skilled craftsmanship of an earlier artisans' republic, further undermining workers' already dwindling sense of self-
respect. There emerged in turn a "novel universe of capital
and labor," where, Adam Tuchinsky writes, a coldly rational
"ethos of cash and contract" left many workers bereft of their
identities as independent agents.[23]

No longer recognizing even themselves, the workers of

this new urban order had little chance of being "read" by
the affluent professionals of George Templeton Strong's social stratum, either. The interpretive conditions of the city
only compounded this invisibility. As what Tuchinsky calls
the "epicenter of the new America," New York should have
made the changing face of labor stand out in ways that it
did not elsewhere.[24] Fully two-thirds of Manhattan's increasingly foreign-born labor force was employed on a rotating
basis at unskilled, fast-paced, high-turnover jobs as of 1855,
and "work, work, work" became the "everlasting routine
of everyday life," as one Scottish immigrant remarked.[25] If
public displays of work were not quite ubiquitous ("visible
continuous labor" is how one observer characterized the age
in retrospect), then would-be workers were.[26] In his antebellum lecture "Coming to the City," the New York newspaperman Horace Greeley noted that "the greater number"
of the nation's cities "are constantly crowded with surplus laborers, vainly seeking employment and underbidding each
other in the eager strife for it, until thousands can hardly
sustain life on the scanty reward of their exertions."[27] But
no matter how obvious were these outward signs of modern
times, a reader such as George Templeton Strong learned
to avert his eyes from what he regarded as any insufferable
indication of his city *at work*. Nonresponse was one of his
perceptual strategies for coping with such unpleasantness.
Simply minding his business was another. For in lieu of the
occasional high-profile work stoppage or street demonstra-
tion — in which native-born urban workers vociferously and
at times violently displaced their grievances on racial and
ethnic "others" — the era's so-called labor problem failed to
garner much attention outside the ranks of workers, save for
those few fellow travelers who remained loyal to what must
have seemed a lost cause.[28]

When they were read as a formal abstraction, the urban

cultures of work, class, and the inseparable relation between them assumed the airy quality of a marked absence in the text of the city. It was easy for an urban formalist like Strong to overlook this absence, since he'd effectively manufactured it. Strong himself, for example, never much bothered with the "essential ambiguity" that Raymond Williams believes characterizes the very concept of class, which is at once a categorical grouping, a comparative ranking, and a measure of socioeconomic standing. Instead, Strong practiced the surface-oriented formalism that Sharon Cameron says "empties the landscape" of all obstacles to interpretation, "so that consciousness can expand." Strong's own perceptual expansion came at the expense of the city's working classes, whose sweaty physical role in keeping New York's basic life-supporting services operational he felt inhibited his untroubled conception of a city that, for him, had somehow been spared the need to tend to the untidy requirements of human maintenance. The form of the city Strong preferred was ornamental, not functional. He might have found reading in the meaningful absence of class to be formally satisfying, yet it led to his relinquishing any *working* appreciation of the city.[29]

The principle behind this practice applied even close to home. As Strong approached full adulthood, his family revised their domestic arrangements to afford their son a greater freedom commensurate with his age. They therefore began, in April 1843, the construction of what Strong calls a "back building," which he would occupy alone upon its completion (*DGTS* I, 200: April 14, 1843). Building proceeded slowly because of a rainy spring. But with weather improving, Strong could write as follows come mid-May: "My villa, bungalow, *schloss*, *château*, or whatever may be its appropriate name, progresses well. It's quite independent of weather now, for the roof's on and they're nailing up lath

vehemently" (I, 203–4: May 17, 1843). Innocuous enough
in its simple relation of "progress," Strong omits to name a
progressive engine, a driving force behind the rising edifice
of domestic form. Not only is his "bungalow" "independent
of weather." It has been removed (grammatically, logically,
narratively) from its maker, becoming a predicate without a
subject. Suddenly "the roof's on," but no one's credited with
its laying. Now "they're nailing up lath vehemently," but we
must infer who this energetic "they" are, over and above
any particulars (when? where? how? why? how much?) that
would further explain their anonymous "nailing." We are at
best invited into the laboring life of the scene *in medias res*.
At worst we've missed out altogether on a foundation making, which reaches us only after the completed act.

All that's left for us to do is to read the end result.
"G. T. S." relates his literary history of "*château*" Strong
in parodic tetrameter meant to recall the opening lines of
Samuel Taylor Coleridge's 1797 poem "Kubla Khan" (pub-
lished in 1816 with the opening lines, "In Xanadu did Kubla
Khan / A stately pleasure dome decree"):

> In Greenwich Street did G.T.S.
> A stately backbuilding decree,
> Where clear the Croton Water ran
> Up to the third storie.
> So *x* square feet of useless ground
> With fair brick walls were girdled round.

Recounted in the diarist's parody is a brief but resonant
interlude in the life of Strong's Manhattan. The feigned
grandeur of the speaker's "stately decree" figures yet another example of the kind of discomfiting juxtaposition of
city living with which Strong generally took exception, with
the "backbuilding" of line 2 falling somewhat short of the
usual lofty heights of poetry. This lyric is determined to sport

while others work, and it accomplishes its unstated aim with a whimsical admixture of the sublime and the ridiculous. The "Croton Water" of line 3 — a local reference to the city's then-recent introduction of indoor plumbing — provides an additional suggestion of the poem's general rhetorical drift. A labor-saving device as much as it was, in Strong's words, "a real luxury," the novelty of "our new bath room" allowed the reader/writer to forgo his regular trips to the city's public baths in favor of an "amphibious life at home," where by July he could be found "paddling in the tub every night and constantly making new discoveries in the art and mystery of ablution" (*DGTS* I, 210: July 9 and 15, 1843). Once again, the work supporting such indulgences has been forgotten, the passive construction "were girdled round" more or less deconstructing the labor behind the rising "fair brick walls" that house Strong's private pleasure chamber.

It's a memorable instance of Strong's reading the modern city, the hard work behind whose construction this reader would rather rhyme than fully acknowledge. Strong underscores his preference for urban abstraction with a tongue-in-cheek exegesis of his own poem. Here he is in the same diary entry as before, pretending to reflexively close read his city reading, much as Coleridge does with the explanatory author's note he included with the original poem, "Kubla Khan":

Errors excepted, viz. for "third" read — *meo periculo* — "second," there being no third story in *rerum natura*, at least not in the backbuilding, and the contemplated bath room being in the second. And for the *x* read the correct number of square feet, which that unknown quantity is intended to symbolize, and which if inserted would convert a harmonious iambic dimeter into a choliambic pentameter hyper-

paralytic with a "tail out of joint" like Pope Alexander's wounded Alexandrine Snake.

The bath room! *"C'set un notion magnifique —
supairbe!"*

Part of Strong's critique is meant to set the domestic record
straight. His "backbuilding" lacks a third floor, for example,
and he would see "the correct number of square feet . . .
inserted" into a reworked reading of his personal corner of
urban space. This is the Strong who would be free from
"Errors," the Strong who, eight years on, could express his
belief that "if one looks at facts, [it] would be rather more of
an achievement than the writing another Iliad" (*DGTS* II,
57: July 7, 1851). An equal part of Strong's reminders to an
imagined reader pertains to the way he has self-consciously
stylized his city reading. To supply a numeric "x" for square
footage would alter the poem's meter and with it a meaning
that inheres for Strong in rhythm itself. A New York of "harmonious iambic dimeter" would be one kind of city; Manhattan as "choliambic pentameter hyper-paralytic" must
read as an alternate urban experience — presumably, one
with a "'tail out of joint,'" in the manner of the Augustan
poet Alexander Pope's favored twelve-syllable alexandrine
line. But no matter its meter, Strong's rhythmic reading of
the city is, at last, an overly formalized reading. Strong versi-
fies his way toward "fact" only by suppressing with his insular
lyrical practice the interest in "social lives" and "everyday"
relatedness that Michael Cohen and Catherine Robson, respectively, attribute to modern poetry.[30] Dislodged from his
native library, Strong felt momentarily thrown into "chaotic
disorder" (I, 215: October 20, 1843). Restored to a formalist
condition of disconnection, he can once more write with
Sunday complacency on October 8, "So here I am, fairly
established in great in this, my new abiding place, with a

long row of book-shelf upon shelf of the great and mighty
of past days looking down on me." Poised, then, to begin
his life's work in earnest, Strong raises a figurative toast to
text: "Health to the New Library. May it witness neither folly
nor frivolity nor inaction; may it be the scene . . . of a quiet
and diligent and steady effort for knowledge and strength to
fulfill the duties set before me" (I, 214–15: October 8, 1843).

If Strong's formalism belongs to a tradition with a venera-
ble past, it was also well fitted for the exigencies of his present
moment. The "absorption in reading" that Robert Darnton
traces to the late Enlightenment, like the "absorbing interest" Steven Knapp dates to the philosophy of Plato, recalls
a long-standing problem of interpretation in the West that
Strong more or less embodies. "What does it mean," Knapp
asks, to be "*more* interested in a representation than in what
it represents . . . in a story than in what the story is about, in
a poem than in what it imitates, in a symbol than in what the
symbol ostensibly refers to?" Strong's habits of interpretation
recall this conundrum and, as Darnton predicted, occasionally led our unheeding reader to the point where "living
cannot be distinguished from reading." Inasmuch as he accepted the smiling surface of the city as his text, Strong up-
dated the interpretive tradition I've just described, while he
continued to lose sight of the city in his undisguised delight
with its literatures. As Knapp explains, an excessive response
to "aesthetic representation comes at the expense of an interest in the very objects to which the representation might
seem to direct one's attention." Strong did not ignore the text
of his Manhattan, far from it. He read his way around it in
literary lines that seemed to him a meaningful replacement
for the "real." And in that oblique act, Strong upheld the
"boundaries" that Immanuel Kant (whose "*Critick* [*sic*] *of
Pure Reason*" sat proudly on his bookshelf) identifies with
the "Beautiful . . . form of the object." With the right literary

forms in front of him, in other words, a reader of the world like Strong was prepared to enjoy the "universal satisfaction" that Kant associates with "restful contemplation." Strong was not unlike the "man of strong . . . susceptibilities," as a nineteenth-century writer in *Arcturus* maintained, a man who had seen fit to "wrap himself up in various allowable luxuries." For George Templeton Strong, the greatest "luxuries" of all were the words that redeemed for him what he otherwise took to be a formless city.[31]

2
Reading the Urban Form of Fire

Cities. Burn. Very. Often?
— MICHAEL B. KATZ, *Why Don't American Cities Burn?*

Few city readers would have been able to escape (or would have wanted to) the hard material reality of the metropolis in the nineteenth century. Not only did they stop and watch whenever there was a city on fire; many of them instinctively recognized that the sensational appearance of a burning block of buildings, say, and the emergency response it prompted were well and truly worthy of their attention. The form a fire took was as much of a "text" as the urban context that contained it. And, like most such texts, the fires that in those days were known as "conflagrations" were open to a range of interpretations. Some readers were held spellbound by the brilliant pyrotechnic displays that the most powerful fires generated. For others, the life-and-death overtones of simply bearing witness to a fire were a matter-of-fact reminder of the high stakes that city reading sometimes in-

volved. In the event that there was a fire to read, variant readings were often in play, for any given reader. These readers
were, after all, trying to subject something that could literally kill them to the steadying rituals of response they normally reserved for their lower-stakes encounters with their
immediate surroundings. A little interpretive inconsistency
was to be expected under such conditions.

That the big-city blaze was readable at all has been much
commented upon by scholars, but seldom have fire's *formal*
properties centered the conversation on what Carl Smith
calls the phenomenal "shape" of urban conflagration.[1] Just
such a reading is proposed here. The point of departure for
this discussion is Walter Benjamin's call for a way of seeing
"objects in which . . . the truth comes forth at its densest."
Or, in an updating of what Benjamin described as a "materialist" mode of reading, we might key the interpretive work
that's involved with fire reading to the "radically relational"
conception of urbanism that Ignacio Farías recommends in
applying actor-network theory (ANT) to the wider field of
urban studies.[2] In the introduction to his coedited volume
*Urban Assemblages: How Actor-Network Theory Changes
Urban Studies* (2010), Farías proposes to "decenter" the traditional objects of urban studies by attending to the "socio-
technical networks, hybrid collectivities and alternative
topologies" that comprise modern urban life. To this end,
Farías advances the notion of "urban assemblages in the
plural form" as a way "to grasp the city anew . . . as a multiplicity of processes of becoming."[3] From this "networked"
perspective, the rash of conflagrations that Western peoples
experienced in the nineteenth century were not only a tes-
tament to the city's physical vulnerabilities; they were occasions of pure connectedness whereby a promiscuous mixing
of persons, communal processes, and human and non-
human exchanges announced itself in ways that might not

have been possible under ordinary circumstances. Historically, there is every reason to resort to fire as a centerpiece to understanding the instabilities of urban modernity. As a question of historical *method*, there is equal reason to regard such "assemblages" as fire makes manifest an opportunity to reconsider the relational nature of the city's complexity, as Farías suggests.

Fire was, it bears emphasizing, a basic fact of life in the nineteenth-century metropolis. New York alone recorded 2,500 fires between 1837 and 1848. Philadelphia fared not much better, its periodic racial, ethnic, and nativist riots in the 1820s, 1830s, and 1840s often resulting in outbreaks of arson and violence. Baltimore suffered a ravaging fire almost annually in these same years. Pittsburgh in 1845, San Francisco in 1850, Chicago in 1871, Boston in 1872 — each of these cities withstood not just a fire but a "great" fire. In fact, in the absence of fire-retardant technologies, which appeared only at the end of the century, or an adequate professional fire department, which emerged in a place like Manhattan only toward the close of the Civil War, open hearths, high population densities, mixed-use neighborhoods, and slipshod construction practices combined to make fire a fixture of the urban experience. One local commentator in New York expressed what was to become a widespread sentiment when he remarked, "there is no hour of the twenty-four that some building is not burning down here."[4]

City readers divided in their response to these dire conditions. Some identified fire with traumatic social change and read in the serial devastations of the city blaze a pattern that was common enough to erode their faith in the fabric of urban society. As two historians explain, fire served as a recurrent material reminder for such readers of a contradictory force that could "build a city" as well as "destroy it."[5] Other readers were drawn to a conflagration as to a freestanding canvas, onto which they might project a fantasy of a city that was simply there to be looked at, spectacularly. Between these two interpretive positions was a possible hybrid reading, too, in which the heavily freighted physical fact of a fire could be partially reconciled with its dazzling aesthetic effects. These last readings hint at the interpretive consolations that formalism, as a practice, sometimes provided. In the examples of what I'm calling "fire reading" that follow, the people who lingered to watch a fire run its usual destructive course were not always conscious of the ethical (let alone perceptual) implications that lay behind their decision to do so. In fact, the decision to watch was less an elective choice than a visceral response to a phenomenon that demanded their on-the-spot attention. What the formal bases of such encounters afforded readers was a weirdly reassuring sense that a city, even under extremity, remained open to their interpretations.

The Meaning of Fire Reading

In fire, city readers confronted some ugly truths about modernity. They might have liked to believe that the urban forms they knew best were unchangeable and fully explainable. But, with the outbreak of a fire, suddenly there lay exposed to them a "set of images" that Carl Smith says revealed the "divisions" within "an embattled cultural context" resisting easy apprehension.[6] Gaston Bachelard argues that fire reading was in no way an "objective" method of engaging with this "reality." Because the "initial charm" of a fire exceeded its "phenomenological value," fire possessed what Bachelard writes is "the power to warp the minds of the clearest thinkers and to keep bringing them back to the poetic fold."[7] Yet readers were rarely, if ever, offered a clear choice between self-protectively recoiling from a conflagration or else aban-

doning themselves to the pleasures of a fire's "poetry." In
fire, readers were asked to consider what (and how) it meant
to make meaning from a city that was clearly more than an
abstraction.

A reader's initial response to a fire frequently marked
his initiation into an important ritual of city living; it also
announced what manner of formalism he was prepared to
practice. It was the witnessing of a fire, for example, that facilitated Salomon de Rothschild's (a member of the famous
European banking family) acclimation to New York after
his arrival from Paris in December 1859, at the start of his
American travels. Once Rothschild had been able, in his
own words, "to get my bearings a bit in what is for me a new
kind of life," he would report by letter to a correspondent
back home that fire is "so frequent here that no one concerns himself with them and not even people in the very
next house are bothered." A fire, that is to say, was familiar
enough a feature of daily life in Manhattan that many inhabitants had ceased to take notice. Rothschild goes on to
disclose that he'd come to have a slightly different response
to these repeated outbreaks. "During my walks," he continues, "I am frequently entertained by the spectacles of fires,"
a reaction that more or less insulated him from what David
Stewart calls "the most feared disorder" of the nineteenth-
century city. No longer "bothered" by what fire portended
for "the very next house," Rothschild now considers himself
free to read whatever, and however, he wants of the city's
"spectacles."[8] This interpretive outlook was not as insidi-
ous as it sounds. In many respects, fire readers were simply
"puzzling out," as Leah Price explains, "the proper relation
of thoughts to things" inside a city that, like all cities, had
always been what Lewis Mumford describes as a "special
receptacle" for the close accumulation of surplus persons,
movable structures, and disposable goods.[9] Mumford's char-

acterization of the city as a kind of repository for the material traces of urban life would have been particularly apt during a decade like the 1840s, when New York saw an average of 1,485 new buildings constructed each year.[10]

Sometimes a reader "missed" the full meaning of a fire by so far removing a conflagration from its origins in brick and mortar that it was no longer recognizable as the text of any known city. Lydia Maria Child is representative in this respect. As an antebellum reformer, author, and abolitionist newspaper editor, Child brought an ethical imperative to urban interpretation that made her sensitive to the lives of all city peoples. She was the best intentioned of readers. At the same time, and as Child reveals in her popular published series *Letters from New-York* (1843), she was not immune to the formal appeal of a fire's incandescent aesthetics. She could be so beguiled by the sights and sounds and energy radiated by a fire that she was left fumbling for just the right metaphor in rendering her impressions on the page. She was, then, as attuned to what was "beautiful" about a fire as to what such a spectacle cost, both in terms of the human suffering it caused and the damage it inflicted on a city's infrastructure. When Child, for example, interrupts a letter to her readership in April 1842 to ask (and instruct) us to read what she calls "one of the most disastrous conflagrations that have occurred for a long time," she exhibits a gleeful feeling of release. "Were you ever near enough to a great fire to be in immediate danger!" she exclaims, seizing hold of this delicious interval to enjoy a brief reprieve from the intensity of her engagement with the scene in front of her. "If you were not, you missed one form of keen excitement, and awful beauty." Child goes on to relate the story behind what amounted, for her, to an ongoing thrill. In her telling, the week previous, "a spark from a furnace falling on the roof of a wheelwright's shop" at the corner of Chrystie Street had quickly raged out of control because the "roofs were dry, and the wind was blowing a perfect March gale." Attempts to resist "the rapidity of the work of destruction" are futile and inevitably fail. Child hardly seems sorry, despite the fire's being "not far from our dwelling." Indeed, while "blazing shingles . . . came flying through the air, like a storm in the infernal regions," and "soon kindled our roof," Child manages to retain enough poise to admit to the "beauty" that's been kindled by the blaze. The "block opposite" even appears in her version of what transpired a "sheet of fire" straight from the biblical book of Revelation.[11]

No doubt Child's excitement derived in part from her chosen genre. The newspaper readers of her original "Letters," which appeared serially in Child's *National Anti-Slavery Standard* during her stay of several years in New York, would have expected a certain descriptive largesse with their subscriptions. In her extravagant retelling, however, Child's formal enthusiasms have gotten the better of her. It is not the moral depth of her fervor but the surprising lack of it that informs this casual sermon turned sketch. Mostly the writer ends up subordinating fire's socially constructed meanings to a form that's lost its objective correlative. This not to say that Child renders fire materially meaningless; she does register enough of the physical city in her description to convince readers they've been handed more than the heated musings of her imagination. Still, Child predicts that "the utilitarian and the moralist will rebuke this record, and remind me that one hundred houses were burned, and no less than two thousand persons deprived of shelter for the night" (70–71). To this objection she replies that "this great fire, like all calamities, public or private, has its bright side." "True, it looks desolate now," Child allows of the blaze after it has subsided. But in full bloom a fire remains for her a "most pleasant reality." She writes:

> The dreary sight ever brings up images of those
> hundred volcanoes spouting flame, and of the scene
> at midnight, so fearful in its beauty. Where houses
> so lately stood . . . there arose the lurid gleam of
> mouldering fires, with rolling masses of smoke,
> as if watched by giants from the netherworld; and
> between them all lay the thick darkness. It was
> strikingly like Martin's pictures. The resemblance
> renewed my old impression, that if the arts are
> cultivated in the infernal regions, of such are their
> galleries formed; not without a startling beauty,
> which impresses, while it disturbs the mind, because
> it embodies the idea of Power, and its discords bear
> harmonious relations to each other. (*LNY* 72–73)

If real houses "lately stood" on the site of this "midnight"
scene, back on Chrystie Street, these have been replaced in
Child's responding consciousness by the remembered form
of "Martin's pictures." The reference is to the British artist
John Martin, whose mezzotint book illustrations drew praise
from contemporary readers who'd acquired the recent London editions of Milton's *Paradise Lost* (Figure 2.1). Whether
Child owned or had borrowed the book in question, she re-
deployed its contents in such a way as to leave her retreating
further and further away from the "masses" of fiery wreckage
with which she began. Whatever form Child has laid claim
to inside the "galleries" of her mind bears at best an analo-
gous relation to the city she actually inhabited.

The Formal Appeal of Fire Reading

It is worth pausing on fire's complicated relation to form,
to better appreciate how urban formalism as a *practice* both
depended on and transcended the material underpinnings

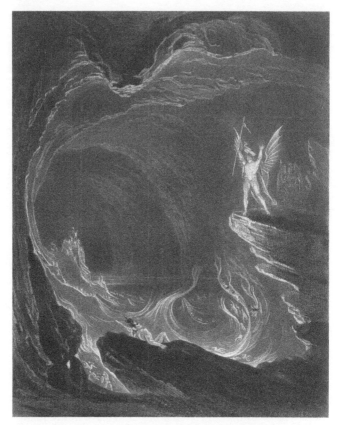

Figure 2.1. *Satan Arousing the Fallen Angels*. After an original drypoint mezzotint by John Martin, from Book 2 of John Milton's *Paradise Lost* [1688] (London: Charles Tilt, 1833). From the Eichenberg Collection, Rare Books Library, University of Rhode Island.

of the modern metropolis. Nowhere is the equivocal relation between formalism, urbanism, and interpretive materialism shown more clearly than in the contemporary response to New York's Great Fire of December 1835. No single reading predominated in the days after the disaster. There were a range of interpretations available, each differing in the de-

gree of material specificity (and air of uncertainty) that readers showed in their response to the impact area inside Manhattan's lower wards. As a general rule, those who were on
hand to bear witness to the blaze wavered in their readings:
on the one hand, closely accounting for the trail of destruction wrought by the Great Fire, as measured in the scattered
piles of rubble it left behind; on the other, experiencing
what they'd seen as the rarest of sensory thrills, epitomized
by the magnificent waves of sound and heat and light that
flowed from this historic catastrophe. The different reactions
subtended by these responses all relied on a reader's relation
to *form*. What separated one such relation from another was
the nature of the mediation (marked by a grim attachment
to the physical city for some and a comparative retreat from
the same for others) that a reader entered into when working
his way through whatever meanings the Great Fire could be
said to possess.

The city's official response to the fire appears as a matter
of public record in New York's daily press. However sensa-
tionalizing it was, local newspaper coverage of the disaster
made the usual interpretive move of both factually reporting and formally distorting the Great Fire, in a reflection of
the typical reader's confusion over how best to read these
astonishing scenes. The morning after the fire, which raged
over two days between the 16th and 17th of December, the
New York Sun ran with the lurid headline, "AWFUL CA-
LAMITY — UNPRECEDENTED CONFLAGRATION!!"
Such bluster notwithstanding, the *Sun*'s assigned reporter
was faithful enough an observer to record that the area's
"most lofty and magnificent stores and edifices" had been
reduced to "a wide-spread waste of smouldering ruins." The
Sun's reporter does indulge a millenarian conceit when he
writes "of the voracious elements which shot its pyramids of
high flame high in the heavens." But, on the whole, by ac-
knowledging the material reasons for the city's being a "rich

Figure 2.2. *Burning of the Merchants' Exchange, New York, December 16th and 17th, 1835.* The artist Nicolino V. Calyo (1799–1884) immigrated to New York from Naples just before the city's Great Fire of 1835. Here he depicts the burning of the Merchants' Exchange on Wall Street, a suggestively reflexive view. The painter includes an image of himself as a reader of the scene in the lower-left corner of this striking canvas. Gouache on paper, 20 × 30. Museum of the City of New York.

and prosperous theatre of a great and productive commerce" and insisting so adamantly in his report on the "combustibility of the buildings and their contents," he takes pains to ensure that the forms that anchor his coverage are more than formulaic, strained, or otherworldly. His forms are of *this* world. Readers could all but reach out and touch these without fear of getting burned (Figure 2.2).[12]

J. Frank Kernan struck a weaker material chord (not a logical impossibility in the city) in his interpretation of the Great Fire. Memorializing the "most disastrous fire of olden times" a half-century after the fact in his memoirs, Kernan in some respects was an unlikely guide to a well-rounded understanding of urban life. Right from the outset he attenuates his reading when he explains that he owes his report to a proxy, an acquaintance who was "sitting," he says, on the evening of December 16, "with a literary friend, about 9 o'clock in one of the private boxes of [manager Thomas] Hamblin's Bowery Theatre." Our access to the "scene" of reading will be at third hand with Kernan and rely on the eyes of someone who may have been trained, like his "friend," to come at conflagration indirectly. As the reading develops, we are furthermore told through Kernan's stand-in that "Science" has yet to "find out" where lies the "mysterious power" of such "flickering flashes of bright flame" as engulf the Tontine Coffee House on Water and Wall Streets, which he monitors from the rooftop deck of an adjacent building. Already, then, we might be excused for believing that city reading, materially speaking, has gotten off to a rather inauspicious start.

Kernan's observer proceeds to a place I'd name (bad) poetry. His descriptions are lavish, his diction overly intricate. His narration is twisted, a study in indirection that ends with this impossible tribute to the most ethereal of urban disasters: "Clouds of smoke, like dark mountains suddenly rising into the air, were succeeded by long banners of flame, rushing to the zenith, and roaring for their prey. Street after street caught the terrible torrent, until acre after acre was rolling and booming, an ocean of flame." The fire that he describes is not an actual "dark mountain," although our reader would have it appear like one as the ostensible object of his attention recedes behind a surfeit of stock phrases. What emerges is the image of a city that's been emptied. For fire, we get the bombast of "long banners of flame." For sound, we hear the hackneyed "rolling and booming" of a "terrible torrent." For sky, we look to a magisterial "zenith" overhead. For firm ground, we roll adrift on a baroque "ocean of flame." The "friend" of Kernan's acquaintance may have seen the Great Fire. We don't, really, when we receive it through such a reading as this. Without a sturdy grounding in the material conditions from which it arose, the Great Fire has become the flimsiest of rhetorical forms.[13]

A Laborless Theory of Conflagration

For the volunteer firemen who fought it, any fire with which they came into contact elicited a *bodily* response that expanded the meaning of city reading. The work of urban interpretation in which they engaged wasn't restricted to their heads; it extended to their hands, so that the steps they took to combat a blaze figured a different kind of formal pattern than anything we've seen so far. Clearly the fighting of a fire was as much a manual labor as it was a mental one, and volunteers who exerted themselves accordingly were *creating* forms of embodied movement as much as they were passively receiving them. Thus, the interpretive arc that volunteers traveled in "reading" a conflagration, even while fighting it, reminds us that the labors these readers performed during the century of fire's special ascendance were no more perfectly divided between the body and mind than the work of this world ever is. Indeed, in a modern metropolis that's said to have "no completeness, no center, no fixed parts," the "openness" of meaning that two recent commentators attribute to "the new urbanism" generally would appear to provide a fitting description of the "disjointed processes" in which anyone who possessed more than an arm's-length knowledge of fire in the nineteenth century would have been involved.[14]

With that said, we can read the contemporary "readers" of volunteer firemen in order to learn something about the particular modes of formalism in which the watchers of urban workers were invested. Some of them were content for the working subjects to whom they'd given their interpretive attention to remain the "objects" of their gaze. That they should have assumed this complacent posture makes a certain kind of historical sense, given that this was a moment, before the start of the Civil War, when traditional forms of work had been so depreciated by the introduction of protoindustrial efficiencies and routines that many of the most affected workers had been left feeling all but lifeless. Quite simply, some readers (among the propertied classes, especially) had a vested interest in thinking of the members of the working classes as so many unfeeling cogs in an inanimate social machine. The managers of this machine had every reason to employ a formalism that further debased the value of labor.[15] Practically speaking, that meant a regimen of longer working hours for laborers, minimal disruptions to the workflow, and the suppression of all expressions of worker discontent. Formally speaking, it translated as the patterned equivalent of these same readers' industrial ideal. The form of the work they preferred was timely, repetitive, and orderly in its arrangements, rather than shiftless, random, or in any way suggestive of productive disarray.

Not so the era's volunteers, who were ever ready to defend the vital contributions they made to the fighting of fires. The key to their defense was the animated form of the work in which they'd enlisted. There was poetry in volunteers' motions, for example, what with the rhythm and pace by which they conducted their hearty endeavors. There were spatial patterns (individual or collective, single file or dispersed) to volunteers' labors as well. Firemen not only performed these forms; they were "readers" of their own labors and so played a pivotal role in determining how the wider public would receive their work. Of course, under the pressure of socioeconomic changes (mechanization, professionalization, the reduced influence of organized labor) they could not control,

volunteers had already lived long enough to see the content
of their work drained of much its kinetic energy, as munic-
ipalities across the country transitioned to fire departments
composed of paid specialists. Conscious, then, that the work
they performed was fast becoming an anachronism, volunteers grew jealously protective of the reception accorded the
most spontaneous forms that their labors took.

They have been aided, in recent years, by social historians who emphasize the most physical aspects of fighting
fire in the period.[16] These commentators often equate muscular prowess with cultural power inside what they portray
as a predominantly working-class milieu, where the decline
of the traditional crafts led manual laborers to search for a
palliative substitute for the independent self-worth that had
been denied them by their reduced economic fortunes.
"Manly" display was one such substitute, and volunteer fire
departments provided an arena where this recovery work
could occur. From the early American colonial period, all
adult male citizens were expected to respond to a fire alarm,
much as they would to a militia muster. This system (or lack
thereof) was effective enough in small and rural locales; in
cities it was less successful, more buildings making bigger
blazes that were not so easily contained by an improvised
response. Thus, the urban fight against fire was frequently
overseen by an appointed warden. Even this organizing
measure proved insufficient. So, during the eighteenth century, American cities instituted regulatory and standardizing
approaches to maximize the efficiency and effectiveness of
volunteers' labor. Central to this development was the proliferation of volunteer fire companies: This occurred in places
like New York, Philadelphia, and Boston during the first
three decades of the next century. By 1835 (the year of the
Great Fire), the volunteer fireman was a familiar real-world
figure in the United States. A fair share of this figure's inef-

ficiencies—the seemingly arbitrary location of firehouses, the partisan defense of some neighborhoods at the expense of others, intercompany rivalries among firemen, and public (that is, drunken) rowdiness—proved endemic to urban voluntarism and would persist as an obstacle to firemen's labors in some places until at least the close of the Civil War. Alongside these drawbacks there were seeming benefits to voluntarism as well. Most important, volunteers made the fighting of fires an increasingly specialized labor, a result of the relative independence, self-governance, and solidarity that their coordinating efforts entailed.

Volunteers might have gone unpaid, but only in the strictest of economic terms. "The work" was "not one performed for wages; nor was their time of labor marked from sun to sun, or from certain hours," as one "Old Fire Laddie" explained. When a city, Herbert Asbury writes, sounded its alarm, a fireman was "expected to stop whatever he was doing, whether work or play, and hasten to a conflagration."[17] To this day scholars disagree as to which trades firemen would have left off in answering a conflagration's call. Well into the early national period a mixed assemblage of artisans, white-collar clerks, and middle-class professionals would have been the standard in much of the country. This pattern reappeared in cities like Baltimore, St. Louis, and San Francisco in the postbellum period.[18] But the antebellum trend in the country's largest cities was toward volunteer fire departments composed mainly of the consolidating working classes. In Manhattan, for example, an enthusiastic contemporary would claim that "the majority of the force was made up of hardy mechanics." These men of muscular occupations, our commentator continues, "when the toil of the day was over, made the engine house a rendezvous . . . above all to be in readiness to respond with a will to the first stroke of the City Hall bell"—that latter sound being the accepted aural signal for many years in New York of the outbreak of a fire.[19] Irrespective of their class (or their consciousness of the same), firemen ran themselves ragged when the city's call came.

Volunteer response was a rudimentary form of work. Tame fires could be extinguished with a bucket or two of water, applied without discretion. Larger and more inaccessible fires (located on narrow side streets or on the upper stories of taller buildings) offered a different proposition and often required the mechanical aid of two or three fire engines. Unbridled conflagrations were a different kind of work altogether; these called out firemen and their machines in numbers for what usually proved a protracted battle. It should be stressed that volunteers well appreciated how indispensable were their engines, those mobile, wheeled water supplies that came with an attached spraying apparatus. Yet the fight against fire ultimately relied on volunteers' own manpower, of which they were well aware. Before the introduction of steam power (more on which later), fire engines were worked manually and strenuously. It was typical for a municipal fire department to be subdivided into engine companies, hook-and-ladder companies, and hose companies, with young male hangers-on ("runners," they were called) affiliated with each for the performance of menial tasks. Given the intensity of the labor involved, engine companies far outnumbered the rest, and with good reason. Alvin F. Harlow, reminiscing on *Old Bowery Days* (1931) in Manhattan, explains how the pattern of this work was read by the appreciative witness. "In the palmy days of the volunteer department," he writes, "each engine was simply a big pump worked by twenty brawny men, ten at each of the two long bars called, for some unfathomable reason, 'brakes,' along either side."[20] This was "heavy and cumbersome" work, Asbury remarks in a sympathetic reading, over which the volunteer "bent his weary back and strained his aching muscles."[21] Such labors only intensified in the case of a major conflagration.

From the volunteers' perspective, what was perhaps still more gratifying than their work was the formal attention it inspired. Writing in his *History of the New York Fire Department* (1887), Augustine Costello draws on the conventions of classical formalism to show the men of his city "working in line at a fire when the flames were aggressive." If the linear, column-like patterns of volunteers court high praise from Costello, he's also retained a reverent appreciation for the heavy corporeality of motion, muscle, and physical matter that characterized the fights they waged against fire.

> I can see the line now, hear the stentorian shouts of the foreman, the uproar of the voices generally, the pounding of the rapidly moving breaks, and other noises incident to a fire. A fire breaks out in Beekman Street, above Cliff. The bells sound the alarm; out rolls the engine, and down they go, the first making for the dock, where they are wheeled about, the wheels against the string-piece of the dock. Two men jump to each side of the engine, unbuckle the suctions (of sole leather, the baskets of brass) and screw them to the tail of the engine. By the time this is done, the "butt" [end of hose] is unbuckled and the hose reeled off by two or three members, who start with it up the street, dragging its length (200 feet) not slowly along by any means, the man first at the engine house and the first man at the tongue being entitled to hold the butt into the engine which is to take the water from the one on the dock, a rule with all companies.
>
> By the time these movements were effected another engine would come thundering down street,

the foreman in charge of the first shouting at the top
of his voice, "Take our water, boys?" "Yes," would be
the reply in most cases, when round would go that
engine in position to "take our water," its hose reeled
off and carried further up the street to connect with
the next engine coming along, and so on [down]
the line.[22]

Much of the action from this passage is exactly that, active.
Working verbs ("jump," "unbuckle," "reeled," "start," "drag-
ging," "hold," "carried") describe a narrative trajectory that
begins and ends with work. The men might be conducting
themselves "in line" with angular economy, but the robust
form of their "movements," whether they work in tandem
("two men") or as a larger team ("two or three members"),
runs in a self-referential circle that keeps the healthy asser-
tiveness of their labors front and center in our reception of
the scene. One suspects the volunteers were equally aware of
the compelling figure they cut. Occasionally, the writer re-
lapses to a passive reading position — "out rolls" the engine,
as if operating under its own motive power, while the wheels
of the machine are said to have "wheeled about," almost of
their own accord. There are, additionally, intermittent examples of overblown reportage, as in the "stentorian" voice
of one Herculean "foreman." But "regular" men by and
large drive this unembellished performance forward. They,
in concert with Costello's place names, clipped dialogue,
and shouted street sounds, represent a vernacular alternative
to staid discursive convention and drawing-room decorum.
Theirs is an experiential urbanism that registers as *formal*
sensation, embodied by men "thundering down street." The
rewards of such a hale, here-and-now responsiveness (of the
workers to their own work and to the watchers who are their
"readers") are plain enough from a worker's point of view. To
the men whom a modern market revolution had all but for-

Figure 2.3. New York's Fire Company No. 39, fighting fire the old-fashioned way. By the middle decades of the nineteenth century, the application of industrial technologies would obviate the need for men to labor away at a manual engine's "brakes." From J. Frank Kernan, *Reminiscences of the Old Fire Laddies* (1885), 87. Butler Library, Columbia University, New York.

gotten, "a combative, physical way of life offered," says the historian Elliot Gorn, "the action, adventure, and autonomy denied in the workaday realm."[23] Fire in this way served as a reminder to the metropolis that its human fighters were a living, breathing form, one capable of pushing, pulling, running, stooping, lifting, and chasing (Figure 2.3).

The accepted meanings of this work proved untenable,

as volunteers became complicit in erasing their own labors as a recognized form of urban life that anyone would want to protect. The beneficiaries of voluntary labor, to begin, found increasing cause to take offense in the frequent fights and masculine rowdiness that permeated the world of fire protection. Amy Greenberg captures just the right inflection of these objections when she writes that an anxious group of city dwellers "read" volunteers' brash combativeness "as evidence that these working-class firemen had their own value system, opposed to that of the urban middle class."[24] More than that, such criticism modeled a mode of reader response that doubled as a kind of materialist critique of volunteers and a community surveillance of their most out-rageous behaviors. Firemen worked hard, in other words, but no amount of urban service work exempted them from the monitoring watchfulness of the most suspicious of read-ers, for whom the firefight wasn't just another form of urban disorderliness. This work represented, in the eyes of certain members of the American bourgeoisie, a brazen violation of the boundaries surrounding the human body. For their defenders, those boundaries marked the acceptable limits of physical display, and firemen's bodily responses were a shameless breach of the emergent urban rules of etiquette.[25]

This critique of their work practices had serious conse-quences for volunteers. As the century progressed, more and more members of the middle classes perceived a need to re-place, as much as possible, men with machines in the name of fire protection. Skeptics maintained that no individual fireman was adequate to the task of confronting the natural force of a fire. The Great Fire alone had demonstrated the ineffectiveness of the freezing hoses and panicked reactions of New York's volunteers. Their "efforts," A. E. Costello ad-mits, "seemed to add only to the fury of the elements," so much so that the *New York Sun* wrote of "the powerlessness of the firemen."[26] In addition, volunteers might have worked hard for their comrades and communities, but they were also guilty of an irrational wasting of labor. Abram Dayton stressed that volunteers "were well behaved, orderly citizens . . . very far from being plunderers or rowdies in the modern sense."[27] Their detractors were not so sure. They regarded volunteers as at best "idlers" and at worst the affiliates of gangs.[28] In either case, they were convinced that volunteers' attendance at fires impeded the work that regular members of a newly assembled modern force were to perform. New York's Fire Department met the resulting calls for reform by barring nonmembers from firehouses in 1836, in addition to proscribing their handling of companies' equipment. Other cities followed suit. Meanwhile, volunteers had begun their doomed resistance to the introduction of labor-saving machinery, the transition to which changed the meaning of city reading. In surveying the work of firefighting, no longer would a reader be watching men match their muscles and wits against one of the more unfortunate byproducts of urban life. They were reading an entirely new form of work, engineered to minimize the muscular involvement of men who had built the very cities that bred so many fires in the first place. The reader of the *fight* against fire was thus doubly removed from the incendiary source of what presumably interested him.

In hindsight, it seems inevitable that industrial steam power, the division of labor, material innovation, and administrative change would do to the fire company what they had already done to the artisanal workplace. It made efficient sense, after all, to trade manpower for steam power as a driving force for fire engines, just as it was reasonable to swap leather for rubber hoses, or manpower for horsepower, as a more productive means of ferrying engines to and from a fire. But volunteers were equally sensible to resist these

"improvements." The fire company for several decades had
served them as a refuge from the industrial designs of the
city's managerial classes, the bosses who would humble once
proud men by subjecting them to the wage-laboring indig-
nities of advanced capitalism. Now this sanctuary for traditional labor had been lost, as volunteers were incorporated
into a professionally managed city — for all intents and purposes, a "machine" — that effectively destroyed them. Steam
technologies, in particular, had been applied to fire engines
in the United States as early as the 1840s. A ponderous seven-
ton prototype duly appeared in New York in 1841, capable
of generating the muscle power of twenty or thirty men as
it produced a steady stream of water up to two hundred feet
long. Herbert Asbury says that volunteers "bitterly resented"
this "contraption."[29] Such a response was to be expected,
since mechanization foretold their imminent demise. Yet
not until 1852 did a team of engineers in Ohio develop a
more viable steam engine model, which soon came into
widespread use nationally. Beginning in 1853, following the
lead of Cincinnati, volunteer fire departments in the largest
American cities one by one began to adopt steam-powered,
horse-drawn engines. Some men reacted by staging futile
bids to outrace and out-pump their iron and equine rivals;
others succumbed to melodramatic defeat, going so far as to
dump their antiquated engines into the water off city piers.

These gestures were rendered irrelevant by the mid-
1860s.[30] By that date, the volunteer system had been abandoned in San Francisco, Providence, Boston, New Orleans,
St. Louis, Baltimore, Chicago, Philadelphia, and even
New York, once the country's capital of voluntarism. Re-
placing volunteers were the paid members of professional
municipal fire departments. Their superior training, technical nous, organizational sophistication, and rationalizing
ethos put laborers in their place and kept them there. No

longer would the fight against fire be a struggle of bodily
response. No more would this work be conducted from outside conventional urban behavioral bounds, the flouting of
which had made fire in a city like New York seem a veritable "revolution," Junius Browne wrote in 1869, such that
"when the alarm was sounded the town was turned upside
down." Fire from this point forward would be managed in
choreographed movement, not muscled in extemporaneous
performance, by men who were deemed unobjectionably fit
to complete the task in accordance with new bureaucratic
standards. Now, Browne summarizes, "instead of being a
nuisance and a nest of rowdyism and vice, it [the professional force] is a protection, an insurer of the public peace,
and a municipal benefaction."[31] Such a "reading" imposed
a disembodied consistency upon fire and the work of fighting it. Before long, most nonvolunteers would consider this
reading as normative.

Alternative Interpretations

As the city's response to the fighting of fire evolved, so did
the range of possible readings it permitted. Volunteers had
always made much of their work's being its own reward. And,
with their labors now falling under the control of a separate
class of managers, they established a pattern of championing
the *forms* of their work for their own sake. It was not that
volunteers discounted the productive worth of their work,
nor had they suddenly decided to subscribe to such interpretive norms as had been put in place to keep firemen's
most obstreperous tendencies in check. Subject as they had
become, rather, to the managerial oversight of their behaviors, volunteers grew increasingly self-aware of the figures
they presented in public as firemen. Volunteers remained
as intent as ever on getting their jobs done. But they also

allowed themselves a greater and greater degree of freedom in the process, the forms of which freedom we might simply call "fun." In short, the liberties firemen enjoyed while they went about their work constituted a neglected (from our vantage, at least) urban form. The various forms this immoderation took thus represent yet another medium for what might seem an unlikely reading of the city, in which a democratic ethos of sidewalk play and an uninhibited exhibition of the performative self prevails.

From the first, volunteers expressed a lusty satisfaction in the performance of their work; they took great delight in fighting fires. Abram Dayton remembers old-timers as "full of . . . frolic." Alvin Harlow thought the fight against fire a "sport," albeit a "rough" one, while Herbert Asbury was convinced that a city's "citizens" only ever organized a district company because they "enjoyed running with the engines, the hose carts, or the hook and ladder trucks." Volunteers' work was not only onerous, then. "Real firemen ran to fires because it was a pleasure to them," Kernan recalled. Other members of the nonprofession agreed, testifying to the welcome self-regard their work occasioned whenever they were afforded the opportunity to stop and reflect on labors that took any number of forms.[32] Some firemen whistled while they worked, for example. Others liked a good serenade, as did one New York volunteer who gamely sang for his brothers-in-arms and spectators while combating blazes in Manhattan.[33] The cities of the United States even paid musical homage to volunteers in the antebellum period with firemen's marches, quadrilles, polkas, and elaborate symphonies that included the use of real fire bells and flames. Each of these "representations," Amy Greenberg says, "made explicit the relationship between pleasure and protection."[34] Meanwhile, such was the fireman's "great affection," Asbury says, for his mechanical accoutrements of engine, hose cart,

and hook and ladder truck that he invariably personified
these as a woman. New York even boasted its own "engine
artist," John Quidor, whom Costello credits with "representing" many "a fine painting" on the shining surfaces of area
companies' engines.[35] Recognizing the commercial appeal
of such images, the era's leading producers of popular prints,
the New York firm of Currier & Ives, ran two separate hand-
colored lithograph series, its "Life of a Fireman" and the
"American Fireman." All of these forms together contributed to what was rapidly becoming a folkloric reading of the
American volunteer as a larger-than-life figure.[36]

Any reading that mythologized the era's volunteer fireman was finally counterproductive, however, to the extent
that such gains as volunteers accrued to their self-worth from
being entered into urban folklore offset their larger goal of
validating the heroic labors that a modernizing society no
longer deemed necessary. In interpretive terms, the most
colorful readings that were made of volunteers' labors thus
represented a self-defeating strain of urban formalism. Trying desperately to establish a more flattering reception for
their work, the firemen of the old school helped propagate
the (mis)perception that they were motivated mostly by a
mindless pursuit of recreation, when in fact their working-
class condition generally consisted of both low pay and such
backbreaking labors as have already been described. With
their fancy dress and tricked-out equipment, the city's original first responders did settle upon a *style* of self-response
that fit them, formally speaking, to a tee. But in owning their
favorite embellishments so openly, volunteers ceded to the
members of the managerial class the right to be "read" as indispensable in the delivery of municipal services they themselves had once provided, for free.

3

The Revolutionary Formalism
of France

*[France's] troubles are not hers alone: they are but
symptomatic of the evils that exist everywhere in
modern society.*
—CHARLES ELIOT NORTON TO FREDERICK HARRISON

There is a politics to urban interpretation that stems, in part,
from how readers make sense of the city's most contested
cultural spaces, the "interrelationships" of which Henri Lefebvre has said are governed by a "syntax" of practices that
constitute a kind of code.[1] The *patterns* of those practices, I
have suggested, might be understood in formal terms, even
though not all of the city's political forms (or the "spaces"
associated with those forms) are egregiously readable. As
Caroline Levine reminds us, "patterns of sociopolitical
experience" exist within a variety of different mediums of
expression,[2] from the unassuming social gathering to the
popular assembly in the streets. Not only are the meanings
of such political demonstrations far from self-evident; they
involve occasions of interpretation that are themselves in-

herently unstable, given the periods of political uncertainty
with which the modern city, historically, has been visited.

In this chapter our concern is with the politics that was
implicit in the divergent *forms* of response to one of the most
memorable episodes of the nineteenth century, the Paris
revolution of 1848. Among progressives the revolution was
at first welcomed as heralding a transformation in the orga-
nization of their society. In the eyes of skeptics, it assumed
a more ambiguous shape, just one result of the reactions
from a wider public (both in- and outside France) that did
not always agree on the forms that political progress should
take. Meanwhile, there was a critical mass of "readers," on
both sides of the Atlantic, whose misgivings about the revolutionary prospects of Paris, on the one hand, and ambivalence about cities, on the other, were mutually reinforcing
in a way that allowed them to claim an interpretive space of
their own. In another context, this group's general indeci-
sion about the modern city and the revolution it had helped
foster might have been a political liability. In the case of
revolutionary Paris, the vagaries of these readers' opinions
became their own reward, so that such prerogatives as they
enjoyed in expressing their personal political convictions (or
lack thereof) extended, by a kind of unspoken associative
logic, to their feelings about what kind of city they believed
the French capital should be.

American readers, especially, struggled with the con-
flicted image they had of France in these years. For many
observers in the United States, the storied French capital
had become a symptomatic figure of what the Boston Brah-
min Charles Eliot Norton named "the evils that exist everywhere in modern society."[3] Between 1789 and 1871, the City
of Light was the site of no fewer than four major political
disturbances that threatened to spread beyond Paris's borders. What had begun there in the latter stages of the En-

lightenment as a republican experiment with which moderates everywhere could identify had evolved by the 1830s and after into a sweeping program of revolutionary change. In fact, by the time of the sensational Paris street fighting of the Bloody Days of 1848, an incisive idiom of class commentary and social restructuring had entered into Western political discourse courtesy of what was happening in Paris, such that "a serious and more practical social democratic indictment," in the historian Adam Tuchinsky's words, "of the nature and excesses of free-market political economy" was soon available to anyone who was prepared to talk the nouveau talk of workers' rights, socialism, and the universal elevation of labor.[4] Before long this kind of combative working-class rhetoric, *à la France*, became a mainstay of a multifaceted conversation on society and modernity that was being conducted in both the United States and Europe. Paris, in particular, from the date of its earlier Reign of Terror forward, was believed by many Americans to represent a foreign species of political excess that they feared was to be visited upon their own nation. As early as 1837, the New York reporter Asa Greene could announce that Paris as a city had been "almost under the constant influence of the mob."[5] This is the Paris that Greene and others sat watching as a portent of U.S. disturbances to come.

There were alternative ways to interpret France, naturally. For legions of readers, that French quintessence, Paris, was a compelling representation of what the American man of letters Nathaniel Parker Willis described as "softness and beauty." This Paris was a place for the "gay and idle," Willis maintained by published letter, where "the very shopkeepers" gave a person the "impression" that they stood "behind their counters for amusement." In a city where, he insisted, "every body has some touch of fancy, some trace of a heart on the look-out . . . for pleasure," the "operas and coffee" as much as "the belles and Boulevards" presented themselves as an "exquisite" public resource that, whether partaken of in person or at one remove, imparted an unbounded "enjoyment of life."[6] Maybe it was hypocritical to have Paris serve as a symbol of special pleasures in a democratic society, as the United States was reputed to be. Perhaps Paris was not, as Vanessa Schwartz writes, actually "representative" of France. But, as Schwartz also explains, the people, politics, and culture of Paris did possess "enormous power to 'represent,'" and what they represented was modernity, the formal associations of which exerted a powerful influence on readers' politics.[7] Indeed, the reception of those associations was inherently political, in its own right.

Urban Formalism in France

Whether one read the city of Paris solely for the grandeur of its beauty or the complexity of its politics, she was liable to "miss" much of the meaning that obtained in between these two interpretive positions. The American author, reformer, and *New-York Tribune* columnist Margaret Fuller provides us with an illustration of just such an equivocal mode of reading. Massachusetts-born and untested as yet by overseas travel, the thirty-six-year-old Fuller had had her maiden passage to Paris paid for by the New York newspaper that employed her when she was sent on assignment to Europe in August 1846. As a foreign correspondent charged with soaking up the sights and sounds and social currents of the Old World's magnificent (and, in those years, politically unstable) capitals, Fuller, in her serial dispatch "Things and Thoughts in Europe," paid tribute to a metropolis that pleased her most refining sensibilities. Hers was a "Parisian world" draped in the "gayest colors," which Americans before and after her have also appreciated. As Fuller writes on March 3, 1847, of her attendance at a sumptuous ball staged at the royal Tuileries Palace, "It was pleasant to my eye, which has always been so wearied in our country by the sombre masses of men that overcloud our public assemblies, to see them now in so great variety of costume, color, and decoration." More than figuring a "decorative" still-life of national contrasts, Paris was teaching Fuller how to read with a certain sensitivity for the formal artifice and ornament that had been comparatively concealed from her during her staid New England upbringing. It was this "Paris!" that Fuller apostrophized several weeks later upon departing for Italy. The French capital had given her a "wonderful focus," she remembers. Or, as she elaborated by private letter several months afterward, "There I found every topic intensified, clarified, reduced to portable dimensions."[8]

For all her French enthusiasms, Fuller also read something unsettling in the city. She had grave reservations, to begin, about national trends in the "modern" art and "Literature" being produced there. Their "main tendency," she wrote of the local hothouse styles, "seems to be to turn the mind inside out." Fuller was consistent in maintaining throughout her time in Europe that "a great work of Art demands a great thought or a thought of beauty adequately expressed." Certainly Paris met any such stipulation for "beautiful" expression. Fuller insisted, however, that "neither in Art nor Literature more than in Life can an ordinary thought be made interesting because well-dressed." A flatly traditional conception of form was, in other words, no substitute for substance in Fuller's estimation; neither "Art nor Literature" was equivalent in her eyes to "Life." "These French painters seem to have no idea of this," she decides, just as they and their literary peers regularly botched the work of representation by confusing "outward symbol" with "interior life" and what Fuller names "the fact itself."[9]

Not only did Paris problematize the reception of pleasure for Fuller; it also led her away from her inherited conception of "Art." Already before her European arrival Fuller had relaxed her overriding interest in romantic aesthetics for a passionate urban preoccupation with society and political economy. In her column for the *New-York Tribune* she advocated on behalf of that city's forgotten classes, most notably the women who had been touched by the poverty, crime, and disease that Fuller attributed to some form or another of structural inequality. Meanwhile, the French-inflected Whig reform socialism of her employer, the editor Horace Greeley, had not only become a part of her mental makeup; it had increased her willingness to translate private conviction into concerted action for change. Greeley was only a nominal reformer of the French school, despite having allotted front-page column space in his paper midway through the 1840s to an American disciple of the French utopian socialist Charles Fourier. Fuller similarly found the controversial Frenchman Fourier's intricate "Associationist" plan for a collective reorganization of industrial life unworkable and uninspiring. Yet the core ideas of Fourier's critique — which effectively marked the modern origins of the social sciences in the West and in the United States provided the seminal "French" concepts and language for an array of period reforms — Fuller took to heart. She took further steps in a reformist direction during her stay in Paris. While there she became a full "convert" to Fourierism, Larry Reynolds says, as she now drew strength from what had once seemed the most tedious of technocratic programs.[10] The change was owed in no small part to the company Fuller kept while she was in the city, for she had contact in Paris with a host of influential radicals. There was Victor Considérant, France's leading socialist and a follower of Fourier. There was also the Irish socialist Hugh Doherty, the editor of a London Fouri-

erist paper. Clarisse Vigoureux, another early follower of
Fourier, entered into Fuller's circle, as did Félicité Robert de
Lamennais, a French abbé and noted socialist philosopher.
There were newly acquired literary friends, too, including
the Polish poet and revolutionary Adam Mickiewicz, and
also the author George Sand, who had of late added to her
body of transgressive letters by writing propaganda in support of the socialist-republican cause.

With Fuller's change in heart came a complicating strain
in her interpretations, as she paid greater and greater attention to her social surroundings. Marveling, for instance, at
the overstocked library of France's parliamentary Chamber
of Deputies, she found evidence of not just a diffusion of
"thought and knowledge" among the whole populace but
what she describes as a counterbalancing "impulse . . . to
look beyond the binding of a book." Reading, indeed, had
become in Fuller's words a different kind of "pleasure."
Thus, she can recognize "the benefits" of bringing "literary
culture" to "the working classes generally," in the persons
of the "hard-handed porters and errand boys" she meets receiving instruction in "reading and writing" during her ap-
proving inspection of the evening schools of the *Frères Chré-
tiens*. Fuller's Paris remained wrapped "in gayest colors" to
the very last day of her stay, which came on February 25,
1847. Yet it marked a great alteration that, by this stage in
her career as a professional city reader, the more conventionally pleasing of the city's spectacles that season put her
in mind of "the poorer classes," whom she recognized as
having "suffered from hunger this winter." Fuller minces
no words in articulating her political commitments when
she writes for her readers in the *Tribune*, "The need of some
radical measures of reform is not less strongly felt in France
than elsewhere, and the time will come before long when
such will be imperatively demanded."[11] It was not just the

content of Fuller's reading that was changing; her habits of responsiveness were changing, too.

Reading Revolution

Larry Reynolds writes that the origins of the European revolutions of 1848 were "many and complex."[12] The same could be said of the various responses to those revolutions, which of course reflected the politics of individual responders. As a matter of historical fact, Napoleon Bonaparte's final military defeat in 1815 marked both a starting point and a turning point in the centuries-long transition to a modern Europe. It was also the cause of several decades' worth of epic geopolitical change. A mere four families — Hanover in Germany, Bourbon in France, Habsburg in Austria, and Romanoff in Russia — had walked away from the negotiations concluding the Napoleonic Wars with their monarchical rule restored over most of Europe. The resulting continental map was a checkerboard of arbitrarily drawn states, thirty-nine of them being apportioned to the Germans, seven to the Italians, and many more of them left scattered and dispersed. National frustrations eventually brought widespread calls for self-determination, so that by the 1820s and 1830s a number of independence movements had arisen across Europe. Belgium separated from the Netherlands. Greece broke from the Ottoman Empire. Spanish rebels prompted France to invade its southern neighbor, intent on restoring Bourbon rule there. And popular protests in Naples and Sicily forced King Ferdinand II to submit to his peoples' calls for a new constitution.

This last episode inspired King Louis Philippe's French subjects to make similar demands. Revolution followed from their sovereign's intransigence. Over the course of three days in late February 1848, assembled workers and students joined

with republican military units from the French National
Guard to march together to the crown's palatial Tuileries
residence in a show of high-profile defiance. Determining
his opposition to be insurmountable, the king abdicated and
fled in exile to England. A provisional government led by the
romantic poet–turned–moderate statesman Alphonse de Lamartine and the socialist historian Louis Blanc subsequently
declared France a Second Republic. Much of a watchful
Europe soon followed suit, with French-style uprisings appearing throughout the region, from Austria and Prussia to
Spain, Ireland, Denmark, and Romania, among others.

The crisis in France came to a head in late spring. For
some time Lamartine had struggled to chart a middle path
for the young republic. Satisfying the contrary demands of
both radicals and conservatives proved all but impossible,
and the newly enfranchised citizenry couldn't agree at any
rate on how to read the "people's" revolution that had taken
shape around the institutions the republicans had created
over the preceding weeks and months.[13] France's revolutionaries were, in short, a congeries of disparate identities and
interests. Their coming together in common cause was a
matter of temporary expediency, a byproduct of their shared
resentment against the bankers and landowners whom they
associated with the previous regime. French radicals (ma-
chinists and small workshop hands, many of them) suffered
a crushing setback with their lopsided loss in the national
elections of April 23.[14] With that loss the radical rank and
file duly redoubled its defense of the controversial national
workshops, which, by May 1848, numbered some hundred
thousand members. Ostensibly socialist communes of a
kind envisioned by Louis Blanc, these workshops in practice evolved into a Paris-area farce of handout factories,
where the idle and unemployed appeared each day to receive an unearned allotment of two francs. Beside these

beneficiaries of the state's questionable largesse stood the less-radicalized makers, distributors, and sellers of the country's manufactures. This faction represented no "proletariat" of unskilled labor; nor were its followers sympathetic to the socialist cause, necessarily. They constituted, rather, a large slice of Paris's working- and lower-middle-class *almost* poor, the craft workers, clerks, and tavern keepers who endured some of the city's worst living conditions. Denied the cause célèbre attention granted the less-numerous communalists and lacking the visibility of France's industrial protoproletariat, the skilled artisans, craftsmen, and petty traders of the backstreet capital's finishing trades composed, like their counterparts in Manhattan, a sizeable demimonde of their own and had an important contribution to make in stoking the nascent rebellion's flames. Sharing their rising defiance were the relatively prospering shopkeepers, who achieved their immediate aims once they had gained the right to vote. Even in the optimistic days of February this class of "keepers" had watched the revolution out of harm's way, safely distancing themselves from the volatile activity of the streets. Now with the risk of violence on the rise, the middling Parisian shopkeepers who had provisionally joined with the revolution in common cause were as likely to side with the counterrevolutionary bourgeoisie as they were to keep their prior commitments to a fragile coalition whose moment of ascendancy had passed.[15]

Differing interpretations of these developments were possible, even if there had been little over which most observers could disagree at the start of the uprisings. February's revolution had replaced Louis Philippe's monarchy with a republic inside the short span of three days. Violence during that time was minimal. And if the "odd, almost accidental, alliance of classes" that T. J. Clark says was behind this transition period comprised a rather "ambiguous" vanguard of

"workers and craftsmen, wage-earners and . . . small masters,"
the immediate mandate of such a "confused mass" was clear
enough to attract much of the middling and lower ranks of
French society.[16] Early signs indicated, however, that the relative calm would not last. By the close of January, Alexis de
Tocqueville already recognized that revolution would rock
France's "foundations." Addressing his colleagues in the
country's Chamber of Deputies, Tocqueville advised against
a complacent reading of national affairs. "I am told that,"
he began, "because there is no visible disorder on the surface of society, there is no revolution at hand." Tocqueville
wasn't fooled by this deceptive display of quiet. He argued
that "men's minds" among "the working classes" had been
"disturbed" by dangerous "social passions." The crown's col-
lapse just over three weeks later bore out Tocqueville's belief
"that we are at this moment sleeping on a volcano."[17] From
that moment, revolutionary fervor spread. By March, February's cross-class alliance had faltered as labor-advocating
radicals escalated their demands for a state response to
workers' various grievances, which stemmed from a widespread decline in manufacturing, inflated prices for staples
like bread, and the pervasive urban want and overcrowding
that were making the lot of Paris's laborers miserable, and
nudging straitened urban populations across Europe closer
toward rebellion. Within this intercontinental context, na-
tionalism, communism, and socialism no longer qualified as
what one recent commentator calls "abstractions"; nor did
the corresponding urban pathologies (and, in some respects,
partial causes of the revolution) of mounting poverty, crime,
and class acrimony.[18] In fact, for many readers of that era, the
"visible disorder" that Tocqueville had predicted seemed to
be coming to pass.

What most of France had been waiting for arrived on
May 15, when radicals led an abortive uprising in Paris. The

nonradical majority of the recently seated Constituent Assembly resolved in turn to drive the perpetrators of unrest
from the city. This plan the government executed with a
June 22 decree, issued in its own state newspaper, banning
the national workshops (improvised labor associations, more
or less) around which street-level dissent had been coalesc-
ing. Young members of the now defunct collectives, the announcement made clear, were to be conscripted into the
establishment by means of enforced military service; older
members would be sent packing to the provinces, where
they were to enlist in various public works projects. Workers
who were restless even before this provocation reacted with
violence. What followed would come to be known as the
Bloody June Days. On June 23, some fifty thousand radicals
helped raise a strategic patch of barricades in the working-
class sections of eastern Paris where they resided. The city
thereafter entered into a wartime state of siege. Come
June 24, government forces began to rain artillery down on
buildings and barricades in these insurgent-occupied zones,
as fighters for the opposition ineffectually shielded themselves with rudimentary weapons and munitions. By June 25,
National Guardsmen from the provinces had begun to pour
into the capital — further evidence, says Priscilla Ferguson,
of both the "profoundly urban character of the Revolution"
and the revolutionary qualities of the "rapidly transforming
urban scene"[19] — to join in the fight against the rebels. The
insurgents' resistance was fierce but unsuccessful, and the
estimated 4,500 casualties they incurred in a brief interlude
of battle eventuated in a contested ceasefire.[20] Fighting
flared up again on June 26, only to subside for what would
be the final time in 1848.

      Americans were as eager as their European counterparts
to read of the June Days' finale, despite its taking an additional two and a half weeks for news to reach them. Initial

reports, compiled in part from sensational press coverage in England as well as statements issued from the French governmental seat at Versailles, dictated how the situation in France would be received throughout much of the Americas. New York's *Courier and Enquirer* newspaper for June 14, 1848, spoke for many influential organs of journalistic opinion when it summarized the conflict at its height. "Communism, Socialism, Pillage, Murder, Anarchy, the Guillotine versus Law and Order, Family, and Property — these were the parties in presence," one of the paper's columnists editorialized.[21] The fallout of this negative press coverage was to foment a veritable "Red Scare" among Americans who either shared or were easily swayed by their papers' ideological leanings. These readers were scandalized by reports of the insurgents' supposed criminal depravity. And they came to share the jaundiced view of the June Days, a view that set the principles of revolution in as unflattering a light as it did the barricade practice of civil disobedience. Under the circumstances, it would have been hard for Americans at large to read France as anything other than anathema to their highest political ideals.

American readers in fact received a plurality of interpretive "texts" from Paris. As early as February, the successful Boston publisher and children's author Samuel Goodrich would write by letter to a friend back home about the first day of mass street demonstrations in the French capital. Goodrich had taken up temporary residence in the city during the winter of 1847–1848. And, as he looked on as "thousands of workmen march in file through the streets," Goodrich was sure the "opening scene of the drama had begun." "To the east," he writes, "is the garden of the Tuileries; to the west are the Champs-Élysées. This vast area, so associated with art and luxury, and beauty, was now crowded with an excited populace, mainly of the working classes." The "masses," as

Goodrich calls them, had begun to build barricades after clashing with French troops. But lest his correspondent misconceive his meaning, Goodrich makes a show of emptying the "scene" of its political content when he states, "A remarkable air of fun and frolic characterized the mob."[22] The American writer and reformer Charles A. Dana differed in his politics from Goodrich. His reporting from Paris was nevertheless divided in its assessment of France's revolutionary prospects. Horace Greeley had hired the liberal Dana to forward reports from the front lines of the fighting once it began. These were crucial eyewitness accounts of the June Days. On the one hand, Dana anticipated Karl Marx by reading the revolution according to the determinist dictates of a class struggle with which he sympathized. He'd arrived in Paris "at the very crisis of the struggle," he wrote at the end of June, and so was on hand to bear witness as the city and its residents "from the lower classes of society" underwent an ordeal of "some terrible confusion." On the other hand, Dana correctly gauged what would be the outcome of all those National Guardsmen and French regulars he saw marching into Paris while he was en route there. This military show of strength foretold a swift return to "security and order," he said, a reading that was as much a formal description of the crackdown he was seeing in the streets (a description that sharply contrasted with his original hopeful portrayal of an "unequaled spectacle") as it was a political prediction of what lay ahead for France. In Dana's words, "In a day or two more Paris will show no sign of the combat except where the houses have been injured or destroyed by cannon and musketry, and all will be as gay as before this strife began."[23]

The recent pattern of France's troubled political history would be repeated, in other words, with the failure of the county's republican experiment. This outcome was the result of a historical form as much as it was a political one. For in response to their city's recidivist history of revolution the entrenched leadership of Paris had once more waged a counterrevolution to restore an elusive sense of order. These "winners" of the political contest at hand had simply imposed a pattern of Parisian life for which they'd been willing to fight. More to the point, they had enforced their own interpretation of the accepted *form* of French society upon a populace that demonstrated at least an interim willingness to occupy an interpretive position *in between* the respective absolutist claims made by the warring camps of capital and labor. In addition to the many human casualties caused by the revolution, then, a formalist practice that in some respects depended upon a principle of compromise — of finding common interpretive threads amid a tangle of competing ways to "read" the world — had been sacrificed to the will of a dominant interpretive class. These last readers were no more willing to accommodate an alternative view of French society than they were to share the reins of legislative and executive power with the radicals whom they opposed.

Formalizing France

However painful the revolution was for the people of Paris, it proved a paradoxical source of empowerment for those who accessed it in a more mediating way than was available to either fully committed conservatives or radicals. For a moderate class of readers, urban formalism was a meaningful interpretive strategy not because it afforded them relief from a historic city's political struggles but because it provided them with a means of adopting a politics of an unlikely mediate position.[24] Here, in the political *middle*, they observed the opposing ends (and the ample spaces between them) of the modern ideological spectrum in the West without hav-

ing to adopt the views or vantage points of either side in
the primary divides of 1848. This was the position of formal
compromise occupied by the New Yorker Donald Grant
Mitchell.

Ostensibly conventional in his interpretive aims and
approach to Paris, Mitchell would go on to propose that
the history of the city's recent trials was written in the most
extravagant forms of its politics. This same politics he proceeded to read as a composite "text" of a city he had tu-
tored himself to know before setting foot in France, with
the understanding that the polar responses to Paris then possible were self-negating in a way that permitted him (and,
presumably, anyone who was likewise inclined) to read the
revolution in such a manner as to arrive at a formal resolu-
tion to a problem of interpretation at least a century in the
making. February 1848 found the twenty-five-year-old Yale
graduate Mitchell tied to a desk in Manhattan, studying
law in a Wall Street office. This was neither a location nor
a vocation that afforded much to his imagination. In fact,
Mitchell was very much a member of that class of reluctant
lawyers who felt the pathos of an urban attorney's life. Mitchell endured upward of a year of that life before he learned
what was happening in France. His response was instantaneous, and soon he'd exchanged his musty law books for a
less tiresome selection of reading, or so he assumed. After
adopting the "Ik. Marvel" persona that he would use from
the 1850s forward in a series of carefully wrought (and well
received) sketches and essays, Mitchell arranged with New
York's *Courier and Enquirer* newspaper to travel to France
and send back "Marvel Letters from Abroad." He arrived
shortly before the violence of June began.[25]

Upon his return, Mitchell collected and republished his
assorted Marvel letters in book form, under the title *The
Battle Summer* (1850). In that volume the author establishes

a host of modern longings. The most salient of these was for a vision of the city in which formal appearances didn't simply represent reality; they were interchangeable with social experience and so made the city knowable as no other kind of context could. Mitchell duly prefaces his dispatches with a dedicatory letter to a college friend, to whom he promises "some scattered glimpses of what had been passing under my eye, during the eight most eventful months of Paris Revolution." As it turns out, most of these "glimpses" are composed of the revolutionary tableaux that Mitchell, the eyewitness outsider, is able to glean from the embattled French capital during his stay there. The writer may recall needing to free his mind "to grow out of its stature," beyond the "city littleness" that afflicted him as he sat down to record his observations. But the perceptual expansion of this accomplished reader is soon forthcoming. Without further delay, Mitchell can relate, "I found myself with pen and paper, bewriting page after page . . . until at length, the pages have become a book, and the letter—a prologue!" In this way Mitchell sets the stage for an account that well surpasses the mock-modest origins of his reception story.[26]

In the meantime, there remained much work to be done back at the site of his legal labors, where Mitchell's consciousness of French politics dawns. It's here that he resolves to trade respectable professional employment for the imaginative play of Paris, and no wonder. The one he performs in what he describes as "the dim office of a city attorney . . . under the cobweb of a tapestry of a lawyer's salon" (*Battle Summer*, iii). The other he chooses to pursue "after the alarum of the new-born Republicanism of France, first came upon my ears." Indeed, since hearing of France's extraordinary February, Mitchell's Marvel "tortured my brain," he says, "with thinking — how the prince of cities was now looking," so that "images" of urban Europe "dogged me in the street, and at my desk" (iv). More telling are the terms by which our want-away attorney conducts his midlife switch in occupations. Not only does "princely" Paris beckon; it calls to him through "page after page" of his legal reading, for which he obviously lacks enthusiasm. As Mitchell/Marvel remembers it, Paris "blurred the type of Blackstone, and made the mazes of Chitty ten fold greater. The New Statutes were dull, and a dead letter; and the New Practice worse than new." "For a while," this beleaguered lawyer assures us, "I struggled manfully with my work, but it was a heavy schoolboy task . . . like the knottiest of the Tusculan questions, with vacation in prospect" (iv). Not long afterward he lays aside his "Chitty" (the English lawyer John Chitty, author of a series of legal treatises in the early nineteenth century), lets go the "dead letter" of the "New Statutes" and "the New Practice" (period reference texts on English law compiled by the Irish-born legal scholar John Frederick Archbold), and comes to an interpretive crossroads:

> The office was empty one day: I had been breaking
> ground in Puffendorf;—one page—two pages—three
> pages—dull, very dull, but illumined here and there
> with a magic illustration of King Louis, or stately
> poet Lamartine; when on a sudden, as one of these
> illustrations came in, with the old Palais de Justice in
> the background, I slammed together the heavy book-
> lids, saying to myself, Is not the time of Puffendorf,
> and Grotius, and even amicable, aristocratic Black-
> stone gone by? (iv–v)

Framing this self-discovery is a choice of reading that our lonely office dweller must make. That choice has ramifications for his present no less than his future, and it relies first and last on his seemingly irreconcilable conceptions of his reading. On one side stands "Puffendorf," the seventeenth-century German jurist Samuel von Pufendorf, whose select commentaries on the Dutch legal thinker Hugo Grotius (also invoked by Marvel) were much esteemed by members of the bar. As a form of interpretive labor, however, such reading was also, in our speaker's opinion, "dull, very dull." Worse, it entailed the kind of back-"breaking," lid-"slamm[ing]" "work" that required him to grapple with his texts and "struggle manfully" with cumbersome meanings that not even "amicable, aristocratic Blackstone" could "illumine" or lighten.

On the other side of this interpretive divide sat France, the dominant monument in Marvel's shifting imagination. At that time, before his landing, he could only wonder at the enticing "magic" of an arrangement of reading he'd not yet known in person, and as a result he devoted his daytime reveries to thoughts of what he initially — and, as it turns out, disingenuously — presents as a "vacation in prospect." Tantalizing "illustrations" of what was to be read "over there" filled his fancy. The twin figures of the deposed "King Louis" and the "stately poet Lamartine" especially fascinated him, as they did many Americans before the Paris violence of June. Here we might observe this sally, in which Mitchell/Marvel achingly awaits the coming day when his most optimistic conception of France will replace his "Puffendorf" with something far more enthralling:

> Are they not over there in France, in the street, and in the court, and in the Assembly, palpably and visibly, with their magnificent Labor Organizations, and Omnibus-built barricades, and oratoric strongwords, and bayonet bloody-thrusts, a set of ideas about Constitutional Liberty, and Right to Property, and offences criminal, and offences civil, wider, and newer, and richer than all preached about, in all the pages of these fusty Latinists? (vi)

At a glance, the speaker would appear to give heaviest emphasis to the most sensational forms of Paris politics. Its "Omnibus-built barricades, and oratoric strong-words, and bayonet bloody-thrusts" predominate in the passage just given, as they surely did in the front-page reports of New York newspapers in that day. The speaker's is no fanciful vision, however. Yearning for a different experience of the political than was available to him in poetic fancy alone, Mitchell/Marvel in fact manages to read revolution in a way that makes it seem utterly attainable. Superficially, the choice that's depicted here calls on him to decide between what is felt or unfelt, seen or unseen. "Palpably and visibly" he nevertheless anticipates encountering "a set of ideas" that can be found in neither journalistic caricature nor the "knottiest" of "pages" of such "fusty Latinists" as Cicero. Rather, Mitchell/Marvel can almost reach out and touch France already, simply by reading of the politics that's freely on offer in Paris "in the street, and in the court, and in the Assembly." It is less a "vacation in prospect" from Latin, this meditative flight, than a comparative reading of "Constitutional Liberty, and Right to Property, and offences criminal, and offences civil." *The Battle Summer* is not a careless excursion after all; it's an interpretive immersion in truly revolutionary forms.

Lying down that same evening "to dream," as he concedes, "of gay Paris streets," Marvel goes on to relate a version of the battle action in Paris that will make of revolutionary remembrance an exercise in social responsiveness. At the heart of that exercise are the forms of a politics that lend a perhaps unlooked-for substance to the style of the speaker's sequence of "Sketches," as he calls the individual installments of his reportage (vi). These he's recorded with a "quick hand" that's relinquished any "interest," he says, in "continued narrative, or the soberness of Historic data" (vi). This laissez-faire approach translates much as we would

expect from a reading that seemingly lacks rigor: It's characterized by what Mitchell describes as the "careless play
of the lights and shadows" of a "stormy summer" (vii). At
the same time, Marvel's reading doesn't just dally with formal "lights and shadows" for the sake of "careless play." His
reading of revolutionary Paris *works* in the way that it at least
fitfully avoids the iconographic representations of the city
that emerged in the aftermath of the insurgency.[27] It's true
that Mitchell's interpretive method saw him placed inside
the safety of his Paris residence once the fighting of June
began. From this redoubt indoors he traced as best he could
what was happening outside, down below the elevated vantage of his window. His response to urban workers' demands,
moreover, might have been condescending on occasion; on
the whole he regarded the laboring members of the radical
resistance as communist extremists. But this is not to say
the *Courier and Enquirer*'s correspondent had missed the
revolution. There's a genuine "I was there" air about his reportage, as if the political impressions he's recorded were
derived directly from the action transpiring in the streets.

Marvel is mostly concerned with preparing the ground
for a more impartial reception of the revolution. This is an
interpretative tactic as much as it is a political one. For in
recasting the extraordinary events of Paris as being of a piece
with a universal *ideal* of the French capital, Marvel proposes
a form of the city on which he anticipates all of his readers
can agree, despite their political differences. He begins this
careful balancing act by revisiting the golden days of February 1848. We're there as proximate witnesses when Lamartine
passes from the Salle du Trône, inside the Paris town hall,
to "quell the tumult" caused by a mob that has assembled
street-side (84). What followed on that occasion has since
become the stuff of revolutionary legend. Our American recalls the urban aftermath, when "proclamations and edicts

have been printed," we're told, to be "read by torch-light in every district of Paris" as "the monarchy is proclaimed at an end" (84). Come spring, with revolutionary ardor spreading, Marvel similarly experiences a "city feeling," or "Paris feeling," that was "too strong to subdue," we're told, "too contagious to resist" (99, 102, 248). It is not that he's failed to appreciate the minute-by-minute significance of the fighting that later transpires in June. In passing, *The Battle Summer* does reveal that the standing French army required just four short months to subdue the rebellion in Paris. Rather, Mitchell/Marvel measures the revolution's significance according to the impact it's had on the *surviving* city, where, the human casualties having been counted, the business of living continued much as it had before the onset of fighting.

As an urban form, Marvel's Paris is, by his own standards, nonpartisan. His perspective might imply a certain politics of settled containment, but it also provides us with what Mitchell believed to be a city around which most readers could rally. Of his beloved Champs-Élysées in happier times, Marvel accordingly asks, "Who has not loitered there of a sunny afternoon, watching the passing multitudes, greeting familiar faces, gazing at the dashing equipages, listening to pleasant chanter or harpist — his soul tossed in reveries, and his fancy busy with bright dreams?" (248–49). Contrasting with this beneficent image is the Paris of June 1848. Here we find that the "equipages are scattered," "omnibuses are full," "the economy has made French ladies more careless than ever of hard-pushing elbows," and the "long range of café chairs" along the boulevards "are empty" (249, 251). No longer "the stranger" to Paris he once was, Mitchell's persona has been "jostled" just enough from his accustomed perceptual position that he realizes some great disturbance has occurred (279). There was once a time when the city's most famous forms (its promenades and passageways, its peoples and politics) manifested in such a way that readers were able to absorb the sights and sensations of the town with the comfort of knowing that the glorious history of Paris, as written in such scenes as these, would be repeating, as all histories do. Since then, readers like Marvel have had to reinterpret the city with extra purposefulness, as recent events in Paris had wreaked havoc with the conditions that once supported a more anodyne interpretation of the urban than was now possible. Marvel's response, as a reader, is to write the city back into a history in which revolution has been reconciled with his mildest associations of Paris, notwithstanding all of the dislocations of June.

Revolutionary Effects

For the political theorist Warren Magnusson, the "fundamental political question" of modern times is what he names "the question of the city." There is, Magnusson says, a way of "seeing like a city" that has been bred by our very urban being. We've grown so much accustomed to such defining features of our urban existence as "multiplicity" and "interdependence" that we can't help but perceive the city in the same way that we've learned to *be* in the city.[28]

What the revolutionary example of Paris in 1848 demonstrates is that to "be" in the city in the nineteenth century (or any other century, for that matter) was by no means to find oneself in perfect agreement with the politics of urban history as it was happening. It was, instead, to be in a position to conceive of urban interpretation as itself a form of political participation, a route into rather than out of the ties of social belonging that we attach to our current understanding of citizenship. Richard Sennett has written (after the German word *Geselligkeit*) of "the sheer pleasure [urban] people take in one another's company," as if the circumstantial togetherness of the collective were elective, or a matter of choice.[29] The disputants in Paris would likely have demurred at such a suggestion. But urban formalists from the past, like urban formalists from the present, would probably have given greater countenance to the idea that a people that perceives together is a people that succeeds together, as pertains to its willingness to secure a peaceful coexistence in the midst of a city's marked differences.

In the end, formalism in France was as much about a city's revelation (of itself, to itself) as it was revolution. Any number of people might have subscribed to Paris as the representative instance of a *form* of politics that validated their most deeply held beliefs about cities and societies. What they discovered there, instead, was an interpretive sensibility — a way of reading, really — that offered them a negotiated way between having the Paris they wanted and receiving the Paris they needed, whether they realized it or not. For most of the parties involved in the revolution of 1848, just having a Paris, period, from which they could reorient their political bearings turns out to have been the greatest pleasure of all. That pleasure was largely perceptual.

4

Photography and the Image of the City

Urban modernity privileges the visual.
  —THOMAS BENDER, *The Unfinished City*

The German cultural critic Walter Benjamin was keenly aware of the limits of urban observation. In his essay "Little History of Photography" (1931), Benjamin writes of an "optical unconscious," his phrase for the new modes of seeing that had been engineered by the perceptual mechanism named in his title after the technology's unveiling in the early middle decades of the nineteenth century. For Benjamin, photography didn't simply make the invisible visible. As Shawn Michelle Smith explains, photography fascinated Benjamin because it "enlarged the visual world" and thus "revolutionized perception," even as it "demonstrated how much ordinarily remains imperceptible." The "optical unconscious" was Benjamin's way of saying, in Smith's redaction, "that we inhabit a world only ever partially perceived." It was another interpretive paradox of modernity, this elusive quality of photography. In opening up our field of vision, the photograph had shown us that our machines and their makers could never register every image that was there for the taking.[1]

Photography's urban orientation has compounded this contradiction, inasmuch as the modern city has multiplied the possible combinations of lives to lead and "texts" to read. This was especially the case during the historic urban turn of the 1840s and 1850s, when the invention of the photograph afforded new opportunities for apprehending the city in the moment of its maturity. At the same time, however much there was to see in the city, there was no guarantee that its readers would make reliable meaning from the objects of their observation. F. O. Matthiessen spoke of the nineteenth-century West's "special emphasis" on sight, evidence for which he adduced in period advancements in microscopy and telescopy, the introduction of photography, and the emergence of open-air painting.[2] Yet despite this cultural preoccupation with sightedness, not a few contemporaries managed to *miss* much of what city there was to be seen. Some of them, in perceiving their surroundings through photography, saw only an image of their own urban anxieties reflected back to them. Others ran the complicit risk of omitting from their life those "pictures" they found displeasing. Then there were those who adopted the metropolitan "lens on experience" that Ben Yagoda associates with modernity. This "point of view" might have equipped city readers to be "electrically sensitive to new ideas, eager for new things to do, new things to buy, new urbanities for living."[3] But it also left them susceptible to a certain interpretive redundancy: In their reliance on the visual *form* of the photograph, they were opting for a formal interpretation of a city that was itself a freestanding collection of forms.

The "problem" with a visual "perspective" on experience, Elisa Tamarkin says, "is that it takes a great deal of control to ensure that we 'get the picture' when we see" what we presume to see. Much that does not "fit" our anticipated "picture" is "deselected or else relegated to the margins" of a viewer's field of vision.[4] Inside a dense social setting such as Manhattan, this marginalization contributed to the construction of what Luc Sante calls an "invisible city." In fact, for nineteenth-century New York's most privileged "citizen" perceivers, "invisibility was a way of life," Sante writes.[5] Rather than see something unsightly, they averted their eyes. Or, yielding to an instinctive need for patterns, they reorganized, in their minds, the visual appearance of whatever required retrofitting. The attendant hazard in the photographic reception of a city was that a reader came into contact with only the most partial of images.

How photography finessed this interpretive dilemma is the focus of what follows. As I have suggested, it was not uncommon, early on, for the urban photograph to obscure what it represented in image form. This is the paradox with which we began: Photographic images tend to conceal as much as they reveal. It is nevertheless my position that the perspectives of the city made possible by photographic formalism were not necessarily obfuscating. Indeed, sometimes the city came alive in the form of the photograph, having been rendered as readable in a way that not even an urban life led outside a picture's frame could match. We will therefore consider a selection of urban photographs from the two cities that sit at the center of this study, New York and Paris, as evidence of a potentially transformative practice of city reading. Our "readers" often happen to be the *authors* of the images we'll consider. Their interpretations of the city (what they did and did not select to appear inside their photographs, whether and where they cropped their compositions, the light and shadow they let play in their pictures, etc.) captured an after-image of their own making. And so, whereas in earlier chapters the forms we examined usually bore only an incidental relation to their contemporary interpreters, who were more the readers than the creators of the urban scene, in this chapter the photographers whom we'll meet tended to have a direct hand in producing such forms as continue to demand our attention today.

Urban Interpretation and the Daguerreotype

Notorious for the lengthy, uncomfortable exposure times it required, "sitting" for a likeness made by the first viable photographic process, daguerreotypy, in the early 1840s was a trial of technology and human patience. From the moment of the daguerreotype's European debut it became possible for the initiated to preserve semipermanent impressions of a targeted visual image using an improved *camera obscura* technique. This latter device consisted of a rude box with a hole in one side, arranged so that an external source of light projected an image of the camera's surroundings on a screen positioned for viewing. Familiar to thinkers and tinkerers in Aristotelian days, the *camera obscura* had long been celebrated for producing a compelling display of lifelike images, what W. J. T. Mitchell calls "exact replicas of the visible world."[6] By the time of the Enlightenment, the *camera obscura* (literally, "dark room") had achieved such currency as to become a watchword for an empirical fidelity to fact. Alan Trachtenberg reduces the primitive concepts behind *photography* to their etymological roots when he speaks to the breakthrough our mechanical ancestors achieved in finally finding "a way of writing with light."[7] The "photographic" means made available by the daguerreotype inscribed startlingly sharp images (of people, places, objects, and other forms) on reflective, silver-coated plates of copper employed for the purpose, and thus became the formative photographic medium of modern times.

Most Americans were more excited about the assisted form of *reading* that photography permitted than they were about its potential as an aid in composing. They were especially quick to appreciate the daguerreotype's implications for portraiture; having one's physiognomy forever frozen on mirror-like glass developed into a popular hobby across the United States. Those who sat for this visual rite — and many did, as the handheld daguerreotype portrait with leather-bound case came to signify a civilized brand of refinement up until the 1850s — might have complained about having to remain perfectly still for some twenty minutes, the interval of time needed in these early years to capture a serviceable image. But for the vast majority of sitters, the relative pains of the process were more than offset by the pleasures they derived from gazing endlessly at the end products. "Reading" the new medium's results became something of a national pastime.[8] This was also the situation in France, where the daguerreotype, like many modern fashions, had been born.

The well-chronicled history of the medium's beginnings needs no rehearsing here. Suffice it to say the Frenchman who is credited with the achievement, Louis Daguerre, after furthering the experiments he'd conducted in concert with his late business partner, Nicéphore Niépce, in the spring of 1838, managed by manipulating the right light-sensitive materials and the *camera obscura* to affix a *plein air* image to a chemically treated receiving plate.[9] Important for our purposes is the extent to which this ritual represented a milestone in *urban* interpretation. From the first Daguerre had evinced an interest in the city where he worked. In the earliest of his reliably dated photographs, for example, taken in the spring of 1838, Daguerre depicts, from above, a busy Parisian street scene along the Boulevard du Temple at eight o'clock on a spring morning. Most prominent in the image are the buildings aligned on either side of the roadway. These comprise a stony architectural frame, clustered around a parallel row of gaslight-lined sidewalks that retreat to the right at a diagonal angle cutting into the distance. Bricks we see, and granite, rising with chimney-top conviction above a hard cobblestone street softened only by the slender trees that intersperse the scene. Peering down on it all are the eyes of the artist behind the looking glass. He's given us the image of a city that has ground to a halt. For where, we must ask, are the people, the pushcarts, the commerce and trade and traffic we would expect to see from Paris as it awakens to the drama of dawn? The long exposure time (an estimated ten to twelve minutes) required to "fix" this image has meant that any recorded sense of movement has been lost to the photographic process. Daguerre's city is not forsaken. It's been emptied of people and their employments. That translates here as a colorless, conventional composition of balanced foreground and background, flanked by what might be a mere tangle of formless urbanism, had this last not been ordered by Daguerre with such care (Figure 4.1).

A second glance at the image qualifies any claims we might make about its depeopling. In the left front of the photograph we discover upon a closer examination no fewer than three Parisians, doing what the locals do of a weekday morning. One man is standing, his left leg raised and placed upon what appears to be the job box of a bootblack. To the standing man's right is the owner of the box, doing, again, what we would expect a bootblack to do. Both men seem to have suspended their movements just enough to ensure their bodily persons were recorded in Daguerre's image. Otherwise, "objects moving are not impressed," as the American artist and inventor Samuel F. B. Morse remarked

Figure 4.1. In this facsimile of an early photographic image from Louis Daguerre, the artist captures the French capital's Boulevard du Temple as it appeared from his rooftop studio in the spring of 1838. Missing, for the most part, are the people of Paris, who have become casualties of a process not yet able to record motion. © Bayerisches Nationalmuseum München.

from Paris in April 1839 upon seeing this daguerreotype first-hand. Back inside the frame of the picture, we additionally see another man seated at a table located a bit further to the right. He is also inactive and shown reading what must be the unfurled sheets of a daily newspaper. Of the three human figures it is the bootblack who is least well defined. He's working, whereas the fact of the other pair's not doing anything in particular better positions them for being visually captured. The limits of Daguerre's chosen medium may have necessitated his "reading" the scene outside his studio windows in this way. But with nothing much "doing" in this remarkable image, the city we see, or don't see, lacks the full-bodied qualities that a more *labored* vision of the modern metropolis would produce.[10] What forms we do see take shape not from the photographer's notions of urban motion but from the comparative lifelessness of empty streets and solid blocks of Paris inertia.

City readers other than Daguerre would administer further tests of the daguerreotype's interpretive capacities, paying special attention to the famed French capital's built forms. The photographic fruits of these labors produced what Lutz Koepnick calls a "proper reading" of Paris, in which the city stands forth in the resulting picture with a dignified grace. "Proper reading," Koepnick says, "relies on the art of taking a pause: on our ability to suspend the pressing rhythms of the everyday and allow ourselves to absorb, and be absorbed by," an "abstracting" alternative to "the exigencies of the real."[11] A couple of Paris daguerreotypes from the period reflect this "suspension." In one we see a magnificent city at rest; this is arguably its natural status, given the medium's aversion to motion (Figure 4.2). *Not* running its way through the center of the scene is the static Seine. The capital's signature river longitudinally intersects the image into neat diagonal halves, with the left (our left, revealing the river's Right Bank) predominating. Up close a lone piece of statuary upon a pediment serves notice that we are in the elevated presence of "Art." Indeed, in the image's opposite corner stands the landmark museum of the Louvre, precisely the kind of place where it is assumed we will "suspend the pressing rhythms of the everyday" in deference to the world's artistic treasures. In fact, this daguerreotype overall suggests the propriety of a rapt response to the city. As in Daguerre's view of the Boulevard du Temple, the photographer's strategic cropping has composed the picture as a quadrant of virtual panels. The architecture massed upon

Figure 4.2. Titled *Le Vert Galant, la Seine et le Louvre,* this image (c. 1840–1845) from Noël-Marie-Paymal Lerebours portrays the signature river and museum of Paris as objects of "Art." Courtesy of the George Eastman Museum.

the river's edge at right, for instance, mirrors that on the left. A viewing deck in the foreground peers out into a vista that diminishes into the background distance, without disappearing. A separated series of transverse archways, moreover, in their functional existence as bridges, similarly fade one upon another into a vanishing point that never quite vanishes. All of these elements lend a formal symmetrical flourish to the scene. As readers we are left with no option but to stop, look, and admire. That admiration may cause us momentarily to lose ourselves in the "text's" impressions. At the same time, our response feels less like an abstraction than the intensification of urban forms to the *nth* degree. What we see is an image that's less a reflection of the artist's vision of the city than a kind of formal self-portrait of a Paris that's been captured exulting in its own *formality*.

Our formal transport into the city is equally (in)complete in another image, this one from the momentous year of 1848. The urge to read *slowly* may not be as pronounced here as it is with the holy trinity of Seine, Louvre, and statue, but the imperative for a "proper reading" is just as "pressing," to borrow Koepnick's terms.[12] This daguerreotype reveals a jumble of closely packed buildings, their irregular roofs and walls an ode to visual imbalance (Figure 4.3). The tattered signage overlaying the edifices suggests we are not in a "nice" place. What appears to be an improvised stone barricade — crudely miming the previous scene's elegant bridged "suspension" of time and space — reinforces this suggestion. Despite these urban indications of dilapidation, however, of slumlike surrender, we have not happened upon a ghost town or ghetto. We are in the middle of a city in distress. If nothing else, the tilted aerial camera angle should tell us there is something "off" with our perspective, and perhaps in turn with the image we are witnessing. But it is the contextual clues of crumbling city, physical graffiti, pitched fortifications, and, apparently, an eerie absence of people that tell us we are looking at the Bloody June Days of Paris. The revolutionaries themselves, for all we know, are there in person, although the picture pretends otherwise. It is possible they are manning that central barricade, except the instrument used by the amateur daguerreotypist, Eugène "Thiébault," as he was known, couldn't follow their movements. What few people we do see can hardly be said to be fighting. They are standing stock still, as we notice when deciphering the dark dots that make a curved, corporeal line in the middle distance. These amorphous shapes are all that remain of the insurgents. Having been crushed by government forces led by General Lamoricière, they stand in broken file along the Rue Saint-Maur-Popincourt. It took but four days of combat for thousands of such rebels across

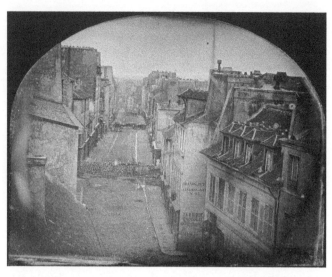

Figure 4.3. Paris as it appeared toward the close of the "Bloody" June Days of 1848, after the government's crackdown on revolutionary insurgents. Taken by the amateur daguerreotypist Eugène Thiébault, this image shows the remains of a barricade in Rue Saint-Maur-Popincourt following the decisive attack by General Lamoricière's troops. Thought to be the first daguerreotype to grace a newspaper story, it is also the would-be picture of a city subdued, of urban anticlimax. Collection of the Musée d'Orsay, Paris. © RMN–Grand Palais / Art Resource, NY.

the metropolis to lose their lives and so relinquish their hold not only on the capital but on their hopes for the insurrection as well. Thiébault's daguerreotype is in this respect a record of revolution that is, visually speaking, concluded yet somehow refusing to end. His image, among the first to illustrate a newspaper story, was included as an engraving in the officially sanctioned weekly *L'Illustration* of July 1–8, 1848.[13] What at the time remained of the Paris press had no interest in depicting the image of a revolution still raging. But, in its jarring confusion of broken lines, slanted vantage points, and slipshod composition, this particular daguerreotype captures as much as it quells the dynamic energy of two revolutions — one modern and urban, the other socio-political and pictorial — of historic proportions.

Because of their unorthodox arrangements, all of these renderings of Paris upset how we normally *visualize* the city. In the first, Daguerre cannot or will not apply a perfect indulgent finish to his earliest street-side image. The impressionistic Louvre from our next image suggests where a city *might* sit, were it not for the fact that even Paris is something other than a chiseled museum piece. In the third, we're presented with a newspaper illustration that would document France's social upheavals as a stop-motion image of surrender, if only the scene it depicts were not so uncomfortably animated. It's not that these pictures have managed to turn urban infrastructure into pure compositional form, human figures into phantoms, or graded shades of white, black, and gray into the atmospheric effects of sheer artifice. They fall short, rather, of any such overly wrought formalism, so that the photographic Paris we've been asked to read bristles with a vitality that belies the limitations of the medium (and occasionally the motives) through which these images were made.

New York Daguerreotyped

A transatlantic clearinghouse of European peoples and ideas, New York was the American capital of daguerreotypy from the moment of the new medium's arrival in the country. "There is probably no city in the United States," the Manhattan-based *Daguerreian Journal* announced in November 1850, "where the Daguerreian Art is more highly appreciated, and more successfully practiced than in New York."[14] Despite having reached American shores only some ten years prior, the daguerreotype had already been extended a most favorable reception. The visual *form* of the city of New York would be forever altered.

Following Samuel Morse's report from Paris, word of the daguerreotype spread rapidly to Manhattan. At least one local man, John W. Draper, a professor of chemistry at New York University, had been conducting photographic experiments at his school laboratory since 1837. Other area "artists and connoisseurs," the *Journal of Commerce* wrote, were still "experimenting in an effort to discover Daguerre's process" two years later, in the summer of 1839.[15] The decisive moment occurred that fall. It was then that Daguerre's report on his "process" completed a western circuit carrying it from Paris to London to New York. Awaiting it there was a distinguished group of artists, scientists, and public intellectuals, who, after translating Daguerre's instructions into English, assembled their own cameras while conducting a citywide search for the right chemicals.[16] In the end it took only until the close of September for the first "American" (a native Englishman, in fact) to replicate Daguerre's method successfully. New York's *Morning Herald* could announce on the 30th of the month — under a banner heralding "The New Art" — that "a very curious specimen" of the "new mode" of *camera obscura* "resemblance" had been achieved on September 16 by "Mr. D. W. Seager of this city." The newspaper furthermore recorded that Seager's image (a partial view of St. Paul's Episcopal Chapel, plus some surrounding houses) could be seen hanging in the shop window of the chemist James Chilton's drugstore at 263 Broadway, where readers were encouraged to repair for an up-close and personal viewing.[17]

New Yorkers responded to such spectacles with wide-eyed wonder. Visiting that unnamed thing in Chilton's store window became, in short order, a trip many an inquisitive New Yorker made, some of them more than once. For the discriminating reader, meanwhile, photographic response was more than a diversion. For this reader, a method of urban interpretation that passed *through* the photograph recommended itself right from the outset as a way both to read the city while keeping its most bothersome visual aspects at bay. The *Morning Herald*'s man on the scene, for example, largely missed the opportunity to include the storefront crowds outside Chilton's in his aggregate image of New York as he hailed the "specimen" in question as "a most remarkable gem." "It looks like fairywork," this newspaperman continued, couching his response in the most superlative terms he can summon. Seager, for his part, would begin to deliver just weeks later the first of a series of Broadway lectures on the daguerreotype at the Stuyvesant Institute. Come the next month, Daguerre's "process" received an even grander stage with the arrival from Paris of an agent for the French business concern that held the commercial rights for the inventor's apparatus and materials and now sought to expand its enterprise in the United States. Before long, Manhattan's first commercial daguerreotype studio would open its doors in the city's Granite Building, no. 52 First Street, in March 1840. Portrait artists who lacked adequate capital were not unknown to set up shop on the city's streets. Far more portraitists opened indoor studios ("galleries" evolved into the preferred term) along what was referred to in the early 1850s as "Photographer's Row," the stretch of pavement on Broadway that ran between Houston and Bleecker Streets. All told, by 1853 there were more daguerreotype galleries in Manhattan than all of England. That same year, there were more on Broadway than all of London. And the word "daguerreotype" had long since entered the lexicon. In fact, the daguerreotype was by now what Alan Trachtenberg calls "a vernacular folk art of the first industrial age."[18]

All the greater irony that the image (and idiom) of photography, having grown so familiar, should have traveled the same road that it had in Paris: a self-selecting group of readers seizing upon the medium as an instrument of high "Art." Notwithstanding the initial talk of photography's proximity to "nature itself," as the editor of New York's *Knickerbocker* magazine stated in December 1839, the visual form of the daguerreotype came to be seen as something rarer than air.[19] There was, in other words, increasing agreement among readers of a certain cultural disposition that the daguerreotype likeness was innately *un*natural, *un*common, and removed from the everyday practices of urban life. As such, "no description" could "do justice" to its "beauties." At least that is how a breathless writer for the *New-Yorker* reacted to the first photographs he saw. His opinions were echoed by others. One, a city reader on staff at the *New-York Observer*, found "no language" whatsoever "to express the charm of these pictures."[20] The hushed, hyperbolic tones of such appraisals did not function at the level of rhetoric alone. However sincere, the awestruck posture adopted by these readers of the Frenchman Daguerre's invention served to position the daguerreotype out of the interpretive reach of their benighted contemporaries. The apostles of "Art" exerted their considerable influence to set the photograph at an interpretive place apart. As the editor of the *Photographic Art Journal* declared, "Photography must assume a higher sphere and maintain it."[21] Joining the new medium there in this rarefied air would be what a detractor from the *Atlantic Monthly* magazine described as the "self-constituted arbiters of taste." For this writer, photography's "jargon of connoisseurship" foundered on "the vagaries of fashion" and "endless theories about color, style, chiaro 'scuro, composition, design, imitation, nature, schools, etc."[22]

These "theories" were not without meaning for the photographers themselves, many of whom had developed classical aesthetic tastes while training as painters in Europe. The artists from this mold might have evinced a preference for such timeless photographic subjects as still lifes, landscapes, and that remunerative mainstay, portraits, but, as was the case with Daguerre, a first generation of photographers in the United States was not insensible to the visual image of the city. On the one hand, historical no less than contemporary "topographical" views of such cities as Paris, Venice, Rome, and Athens had represented an indispensable part of their formal educations. On the other, a number of these photographers were determined to apply their traditional understanding of the urban forms of the past to the modern cities of the present, and they did. The "urban-view tradition" would never compete with the popularity or profitability of portraiture. But, as Peter Hales explains, it was a legitimate "genre" of its own.[23] As a group, the genre's photographers inherited from European painters what Hales says was a stately "grand style" consisting of a "delicately balanced admixture of factual documentation, picturesque interpretation, and urban celebration." Their being "trained to see the city in culturally conservative ways" was not in itself a guarantee that American photographers would practice a rather unadventurous urban formalism. Yet when they put their preferred principles of imaging into practice, the cities they pictured in their work proved to be comparatively flat, even by the standards of the nineteenth century. Hales observes that these artists' "increasingly homogeneous and tightly packed style" figured a "mythology" of a preternaturally composed city. It's true that to fit any city inside a photographic frame is itself an ordering gesture. But to frame such an image in accordance with the centuries-old lessons of Europe, in the face of the vibrant urban life that was then taking shape in the United States, was to insist on an illusionary form of urbanism. Having "made photographs,"

Hales summarizes, "that placed the city within older models of perception," the *auteurs* of the urban view "transformed the new and unsettling world into acceptable and comprehensible patterns." Photography was, for them, a visual remedy for "disorder and its disorienting effects."[24]

That the artistry these photographers practiced would prove to rely as heavily as it did on formal experimentation is only another irony in the city's interpretive history. Among the most notable of contemporary photographers to breathe a surprising life into his visual representations of the city was Victor Prevost.[25] Born in France in 1820, Prevost studied painting in the Paris studio of the noted neoclassicist Paul Delaroche, where, it turns out, some of the greatest French photographers trained. Prevost emigrated to New York in 1853 to establish himself as an artist, then photographer, after he forged a partnership with a friend from Paris, Peter C. Duchochois. Still new to the photographic medium, Prevost failed to meet with immediate success. Uncommitted to portraiture and still unaware of the "niche market" that Hales says the urban view was about to become, Prevost returned to Delaroche's studio for advanced training in what he had now decided was his trade.[26] It was there that he met Gustave Le Gray. Like Prevost a painter turned photographer, Le Gray was by this time an innovator in his profession. His chief contribution to the field was an improved process for waxing paper photographic negatives, a process that foretold a decisive departure from the one-of-a-kind daguerreotype's silver-coated glass plates. The Englishman William Henry Fox Talbot already had done important work in this vein in the early 1840s. His calotype, or *talbotype*, process would eventually enable artists to derive, with some imperfections, multiple photographic images from a single paper negative print. It was Le Gray's idea to wax Talbot's paper negatives, a streamlining process that, if imperfect, converted a number of photographers, including Prevost.

Now back in New York, Prevost not only chose to survey his adopted city through the eye of the camera; he resolved to collect the resulting negatives as a book, capitalizing on the dual capacity for mass production and distribution that wax papering made possible. Prevost's surviving images make no attempt to conceal his feelings about the upstart unruliness of the New World's cities. To tame this "text" he resorted to the academic pictorial aesthetic that had been instilled in him during his European upbringing. It had taken centuries to raise the monumental profile of the civic, historic Paris to which Prevost was accustomed. A conventionally French notion of what a city is reappears in his work. At heart Prevost is a romantic neoclassicist who has held onto a traditional image of urbanism despite having long since crossed over to the livelier shores of the western Atlantic. His photographic record of nineteenth-century Manhattan thus reads as a concerted attempt to image the "beautiful," predictably linear city that he wants New York to be. Those attempts were uneven at best. Prevost's project never materialized as a completed publication; nor did the photographer deliver quite the monumental overview of his metropolis he had promised. This outcome seems to have been all but unavoidable, considering the artist's stated conviction that "in Photography the slightest accident may cause deplorable results."[27]

From 1853 to 1854, Prevost searched the city for what were, to him, an acceptable collection of representative urban forms. Not finding these, he settled on creating (for a wider reading public, he thought) images of New York at its most conventionally commanding. Inspired, no doubt, by the buttoned-up images of the city appearing in the "New York Daguerreotyped" series from *Putnam's* magazine, in 1853, as well as by the preservation efforts of the Mission Héliographique in France to photograph that country's historic monuments, Prevost completed his visual review of

New York by seeking out the kinds of soaring Gothic spires and neoclassical columns, entablatures, and pediments that he had been reared on in Europe. Branching out from his studio at 627 Broadway, he decided that New York's elegant Grace Street Church agreed with his antiquarian aesthetic. So, too, did the Athenian-looking Appleton's bookstore (Figure 4.4). The courtyard classicism of Columbia College also made the grade, and we can see why. The images of Prevost's Manhattan are rigid and upright in their imposing stateliness. Although they were never collected between boards in their totality, his individual photographs are as orderly, iconographic, and inoffensive as he could have wished them to be. As visual placeholders for the image of the city Prevost dreamed of, however, his photographs fall well short of the artist's unchanging ideal. It's not just that they had been meant to be read as illustrations in common, under a single cover; cumulatively, they do in fact insist on being read *together*, as part of an implicit storyline that would account for all of the unspoken connections between the pictures we do and don't see. Received in this way, Prevost's images suggest the outlines of an "urban organism" that is living, breathing, growing.[28] An interconnected network of churches and universities and intellectual trade is taking shape — a modern urban form, as it were — right before our eyes, and Prevost was just about on hand to observe it, in spite of his reservations.

Having abandoned his ambitions to produce a book, Prevost went ahead and issued and sold his images as single prints of an unusually large scale, 13×15 inches or even 18×22. Aside from their size, there was nothing noteworthy about these photographs when taken on a case-by-case basis. But when read as part of a larger collective of urban impressions, they represent a city that's visually meaningful precisely because it's at *work*. The exposure times for the

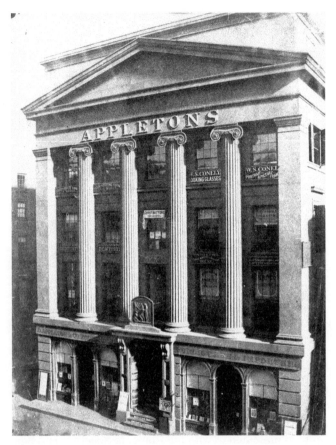

Figure 4.4. A formidable New York monument from the photographer Victor Prevost of the Manhattan book dealer D. Appleton & Co., 346-348 Broadway. Calotype c. 1853–1854. ID 26115. PR056.1.02. Collection of the New-York Historical Society.

calotype technology employed by Prevost remained, like that of the daguerreotype, too long to record motion. Still, in electing to photograph such local laboring establishments as the Fourth Avenue showrooms of the French furniture makers Ringuet-Leprince, Marcotte & Co., as well as Gurney's

Figure 4.5. Antebellum New York at "work," a calotype view, c. 1853–1854, by V. Prevost of Old Herring's Safe Factory, occupying block, Thirteenth Street–Ninth Avenue–Twelfth Street–Hudson. ID 26136. PR 056 Victor Prevost Photograph Collection, New-York Historical Society.

Daguerrean Gallery, on Broadway, and Old Herring's Safe Factory, on Hudson between Twelfth and Thirteenth Streets (Figure 4.5), the artist has made an unintended claim on behalf of a city that's always already *moving*. Once again Prevost has presented us with full-frontal perspectives and rigid right angles, the visual equivalent of the city grid he'd like to impose upon a Manhattan that simply wouldn't stand still.

Other Urban Interpretations

Following on the photographic volume that Prevost planned but didn't complete, artists in other U.S. cities were able to offer their own urban views as fully realized books, only to see the achievement supplanted by yet another optical invention with urban interpretive implications, stereoscopy.[29] The double-image concept of the stereoscope had been in place, and for sale, in Europe as early as 1850. Just one year later it was available in the United States. "Readers" who purchased the appropriate looking device, and with it the cheaply affordable slide-insert "stereo" views of natural scenery, manmade disasters, and the like, availed themselves during the next decade of an entertaining mechanism that reproduced an illusionary world of three-dimensional depth and effect. If we are to believe one English commentator, the stereoscope enabled "the people" to "acquire a general knowledge of the works of God and of man — of things common and uncommon — of the miracles of nature and of art," much as if they had just "learned to read [the] Bible."[30] When, in 1859, the photographic firm of the New Yorker Edward Anthony published its first line of "Anthony's Instantaneous Views of New York," stereoscopy crossed an important barrier of urban perception.

Hales lauds Anthony's achievement as "revolutionary."[31] The new mechanism used a small, lightweight camera to produce correspondingly small stereo-pair images of about 3×3 inches. In mounting any one of these images in Anthony's stereoscope, unique in its reliance on a short focal length to admit the maximum amount of light per square inch of image, a seer suddenly saw what neither daguerreotype nor calotype had been able to represent: stilled images of human, animal, and mechanical motion. Hence the "instantaneous" name of Anthony's New York "views." Moving objects that were located in the middle and background of utilized photographs stood the best chance of registering effective stop-motion impressions. And Anthony had to compensate for the tiny size of his final images by employing a double magnifier with his device to add the appearance of life-sizedness to his scenes. His venture was furthermore

more commercial than it was disinterestedly visual. The two hundred separate stereo views, for example, that Anthony produced in only his first year of operation — the most notable of these being of Broadway, the New York hub that his establishment also called home — served in no small way to mass market his own photographic supply business. Regardless of his intentions, convictions, or profits, however, Anthony revised the way Americans perceived their cities. His widely distributed views of modern instantaneity provided a common-denominator image of urbanism. More to the perceptual point, a single stereographic view from the hand of Anthony was like "a leaf," the Boston man of letters Oliver Wendell Holmes said, "from the book of God's recording angel."[32] Indeed, as a serial collection of scenes, Anthony's images suggested that the city was less a still-life monument than a complex nexus of energy and activity. For "with these stereo views," Hales writes, "Anthony became the first American photographer to propose the city not only as object but, more crucially, as process."[33]

There was a problem with the "process" nonetheless, undetected by nineteenth-century observers. Anthony's New York "view" *Broadway in the Rain* (c. 1860s) exposes as well as any of his images the unforeseen limitations of "instantaneous" perception (Figure 4.6). *Broadway* proved to be one of the firm's most collectible prints, a steady seller throughout the 1860s. Perhaps it was the layers of paradox that made it a must-buy for stereoscopic readers. These, at least, are what hold our attention today. Despite, for instance, its being a "rainy" day, we somehow see the city before us with astonishing clarity. Also, notwithstanding the snarl of street traffic at image center, the thoroughfare depicted cuts through the scene with such forcefulness — a consequence, no doubt, of "instantaneous" technology — that our impression is of fluid movement. Here, in fact, stop-imagery almost assumes a life

Figure 4.6. A crowd-pleasing favorite for much of the 1860s, Edward Anthony's "instantaneous" stereo view *Broadway in the Rain* (c. 1860s, likely taken from 308 or 310 Broadway, New York City) offers a clear but clouded image of a city in motion. Albumen silver print from glass negative. Image copyright © The Metropolitan Museum of Art. Image source: Art Resource, NY.

of its own. This illusion of controlled chaos, of commotion made safe by orchestration, is enhanced further by buildings that vertically bookend the scene at left and right and by the way a lone, umbrella-wielding pedestrian (in his reflective pause, a proxy for us as readers) stands just apart from it all in the foreground, soaking up the scene in its kinetic splendor. It is a visual ruse, of course, since no lived city ever stops long enough to achieve even this semblance of suspension, of synchronic harmony. But that is not to say this picture is only "about" the visual pleasure that comes to parlor-seated spectators who would apply ordered photographic form on top of relative urban formlessness. There is an unmitigated joy in the crowded movement and pedestrian spontaneity of this photograph, no matter the dry titles of some of the book catalogues that Anthony published for enthusiasts in the period, including *Catalogue of Photographic Apparatus and Material, Manufacturers, Imported and Sold by E. Anthony* (1854), *New Catalogue of Stereoscopes and View Manufactured and Published by E. Anthony American and Foreign Stereoscopic Emporium* (1862), and *Catalogue of Card Photographs, Published and Sold by E. and H. T. Anthony* (1862). In the interpretive route traveled from *camera obscura* to daguerreotype and on to talbotype, calotype, and city stereoscope, the urban forms of the photographic image have followed a trajectory from the quietism of still life to the unbridled excitement of street life.

The reader who came closest to seeing stereoscopy for what it was, and what it was not, is Oliver Wendell Holmes. Not only did Holmes join in the chorus of connoisseurs who came to dominate the era's discussion of the whole host of new visual media. He cornered the conversation on stereoscopy with a pair of considered essays published in the *Atlantic Monthly*, since its founding in 1857 a journal that self-consciously catered to some of America's most knowing metropolitans. In the first of these articles, from June 1859, Holmes reminded readers just how "miraculous" the photographic arts were, even if they had "become such an everyday matter with us." Two years later, he followed up on his thoughts concerning "The Stereoscope and the Stereograph" with a more searching formal analysis. Likening this newest photographic format to "Sun-Sculpture," because of its simulated three-dimensionality, Holmes begins by dismissing the complaints of critics who felt that black-and-white photographic imaging was not lifelike enough, whether or not images possessed depth. Holmes will have none of it. "But color is, after all," he writes, "a very secondary quality as compared with form." Holmes does concede at least one virtue in the stereoscope's comparative realism. "As to motion," he continues, "it is wonderful to see how nearly" its "effect" is "produced." As Holmes proceeds, however, we learn that he rates stereographic "motion" for reasons other than its resemblance to "real" life. What's "wonderful" for him about the "sun-sculpture of the stereograph" is that it provides an "artificial contrivance for the gratification of human taste." The illusion of movement, that is, warrants our attention to the extent that it's a "source of pleasure." It is not that "life" as such is of little concern to the stereophile Holmes as he sorts, by his count, "a hundred thousand stereographs" or flits through his "collection of about a thousand." Stereoscopy signifies as long as he (and, by implication, we) can locate in the forms of a photograph the satisfaction of "artificial . . . gratification." This, at least, is Holmes's initial proffered belief, his account of how he can now "feel the same excitement on receiving a new [stereographic] lot to look over and select from as in those early days of our experience." Here, "looking" is "life." "Reading" itself constitutes "experience."[34]

If Holmes held conventional views on visual representation, his city "reading" was also informed by a formalism unmistakably modern and urban in its expansiveness. Upon sorting through his sizeable stereographic collection, he invites readers of his essay on "Sun-Sculpture" inside the internal workings of his mind to witness his reception of Edward Anthony's *Broadway on a Rainy Day* (1859), which "miraculous instantaneous view" (the serial predecessor of Anthony's *Broadway in the Rain*) Holmes happens to have on hand. He reads the image in real time, and sets the scene when he begins, "Here we are in the main street of the great city." It is an awkward interpretive position, since we find ourselves situated amid the workaday world of not just any city but "the great city" that we have supposedly left behind in our "artificial . . . gratification" of this, its representational image. To begin this reading, we are in the middle of "the

main street," no less. Holmes's next interpretive move, im-
portantly, is to carry city readers from an earlier era of imag-
ery to one where they've never been before. The "character"
of the stereoscopic city, he assures us, is "perhaps best shown
by the use we make of it . . . to illustrate the physiology of
walking." And what a strange walking it is. "Every foot,"
Holmes observes, "is caught up in its movement with such
suddenness that it shows as clearly as if quite still." Or, as
he concludes of "this simple-looking paradox," "All is still
in this picture of universal movement." Motion seems "but
a succession of rests." That, at least, is what Holmes is left
believing, or perceiving, as he regards Manhattan in the
light of the stereoscope. He can only "wonder" at Anthony's
Broadway view "No. 203," as he numbers it, "this snatch at
the central life of a mighty city as it is rushed by in all its
multitudinous complexity of movement!"

Holmes calls this image a "metaphysical puzzle." We
might name it a formal conundrum, precisely the image we
would expect from a city trapped between alternate understandings of form. One of these understandings was historically indebted to an inflexible European aesthetic that pitted
"life" against "art"; the other depended upon a metropolitan
future that would only ever be unsettled. Locating all the
"motion" of a "hurried" urban "day's life" in "a succession
of rests," Holmes reads into this riddle-like visual representation of the city a meaning for which he would otherwise
have been at a loss. Instead, his stereoscopic reading of New
York allows him to have his forms and his city at one and the
same time, in one and the same place.[35]

Clearly modern photography was not always the revelation it seemed. Various visual devices had each in their way
shown that a viewer's subjective response to an image was
never wholly inseparable from his capacity for sight. And the
perennial "improvement" of one photographic technology

upon another argued against any observational mode's ever being the consensus choice for all observers. Reviewing in 1850 the previous decade's mechanical milestones, for example, the *Bulletin of the American Art-Union* continued to accept "these old pictures of Daguerre," from 1838 and 1839, as the pinnacle of perception. The publication's spokesman in fact decreed that daguerrean "Art" had "since produced nothing more beautiful in its impressions upon metallic plates." Such image contradictions were enough to draw the notice of the satirist. Looking back on the century's visual presumptions in 1888, the American author Herman Melville would write of "the microscope, telescope, and other inventions for sharpening and extending our natural sight, thus enabling us mortals . . . to enlarge upon the field of our original and essential ignorance." Maybe Americans of that era thought they were seeing more, but they were not, necessarily. This was particularly true with respect to their observations of cities, which have long been susceptible to such various forms of self-concealment as we've seen.[36]

Afterword

Urban Formalism has examined what it historically meant to "read" the mid-nineteenth-century city, in the broadest sense of that term. I've placed *forms* at the heart of this study in the belief that the work of urban interpretation ultimately requires us to attend to the representative patterns of the city's cultural formations. These days, such formations are increasingly recognized as "forms." This study accordingly sits at the semantic intersection of some of the historical city's most readable (which is not to say most easily apprehensible) formal "texts." Among these last I have included the literary city, the material city, the political city, and the visual city. My argument, throughout, has been that the often contradictory ways by which our predecessors interpreted the forms of the modern city at once made the metropolis more and less readable. The bulk of this book, then, provides the basis for a two-part claim. I contend, first, that both formalism and urbanism were and remain interpretive practices in their own right. Within the metropolitan setting that concerns me, the one was as much a means of making meaning as the other. Second, it is my position that urbanism and formalism have furthermore stood in an ambivalent relation to each other from their modern beginnings. By turns they have proved mutually reinforcing and always complicating, in accordance with readers' readiness to make form a central factor in how they engaged with the everyday world.

The formal negotiation of the city persists to this day. As the preceding pages of this study have shown, we have long been relying on urban forms to respond to one of the most complex texts of our times, the city. And, if the attention we have paid to the city's infinite formal variety has taught us anything, it's this: Our confrontations with the forms of modernity need not be confrontational. Increasingly, they're not. Such web-based projects as "City of Print: New York and the Periodical Press," for example, have facilitated our access to an important archive of historical urban reading materials.[1] In addition, current work in the digital and spatial humanities has offered us wholly new ways of reading the city. Legions of city readers are out there, their urban interpretive habits a potential key to the reading of a cityscape that we are now able to map with remarkable accuracy and detail.[2] Indeed, the participants in New York University's self-styled research community *New York Scapes* are not simply affording us a better mental "map" of the city. They've undertaken, in their own words, a "multidisciplinary inquiry into the city's evolving cultural geographies," to "foster critical engagement with institutions, media, spaces, and performances that continue to shape urban experience and humanist practices in the twenty-first century."[3]

But it is not, finally, the availability of superior research tools that makes us better readers of city reading. Rather, we are better city readers because we have grown in our appreciation of the fact that urban forms are themselves among the greatest interpretive resources we have at our disposal. The

French curator and art critic Nicolas Bourriaud somewhat misleadingly describes the "artistic activity" of modernity as "a game, whose forms, patterns and functions develop and evolve according to periods and social contexts." That "game" is the most serious of undertakings, "intended" as it is "to prepare and announce a future world."[4] *Urban Formalism* has attempted to reveal a glimpse of that world, while excavating the historical and formal foundations on which it was built.

Acknowledgments

This book began by chance in Ankara, Turkey. As a faculty member of the Department of American Culture and Literature at Bilkent University, situated in the capital city's western suburbs, I decided (a fruitful decision, it turns out) to test the scholar Perry Miller's claim, made in his book *The Raven and the Whale* (1956), that the diary of the nineteenth-century New Yorker George Templeton Strong was an invaluable primary source for studying the period. Little did I realize as I began to work my way through the four-volume modern edition of this historical resource that I was initiating the research that would culminate, some twelve years later, in the publication of this very book, *Urban Formalism*. Sitting along the periphery of one city, in central Anatolia, I undertook the project that I completed while residing in the coastal outskirts to the south of another, Providence, Rhode Island. Reading and thinking and writing about cities have long seemed the natural thing to do, in my moves between cities.

None of this work would have been possible without

the help I received along the way. At South Dakota State
University (SDSU), I received an award for Academic and
Scholarly Excellence from the Office of Academic Affairs
that permitted me to conduct summer research in New
York in 2010. This time proved to be a turning point for my
project, and I am grateful to Jerry Jorgensen, former Dean of
the College of Arts and Sciences, and Jason McEntee, Department Head and Professor of English, for their support.
No less supportive at SDSU were my friends and former colleagues Michael Keller and Paul Baggett. Michael remains
my ideal of grace under life's pressures, while I have never
known anyone as selfless as Paul. Both are my pole stars of
the Upper Plains. Grant Farred, of Cornell University, has
been the most faithful of friends in any number of places,
including my current academic home at the University of
Rhode Island (URI). In 2013, a Faculty Research Grant from
URI's Center for the Humanities underwrote a second research trip to New York, a trip that helped move *Urban Formalism* much closer to its published form. And, in the fall
of 2014, an invitation by my URI colleague in English Kath-
leen Davis to present my work before our department's Colloquium Speakers Series gave me the opportunity to further
refine the ideas behind what would become this book's first
chapter. Another colleague, Carolyn Betensky, encouraged
me to observe the cultural spaces of the urban transatlantic
from a Victorian perspective, and Mary Cappello, Professor of English and Creative Writing at URI, continues to
spur me with hallway conversations that urge the necessity
of one's writing.

That a book which began so far from my present home
should have found a home at Fordham University Press is
an outcome I never could have expected. The director of
Fordham University Press, Fredric Nachbaur, has navigated
this project with kindness and assurance from day one. I owe

him everything. Will Cerbone also brought much-needed calm to the review process, providing just enough humor to lighten what might have otherwise seemed, at least for me, a difficult path to publication. *Urban Formalism* made its way to Fordham University Press at all because of Daniel J. Monti, Professor of Sociology at Saint Louis University. As the book series editor of POLIS: Fordham Series in Urban Studies, Professor Monti has been standing behind my work for more than a few years now. His believing in *Urban Formalism* has made all the difference in the world for the writer. For that belief I give thanks.

Rachel Boccio read every last word of the manuscript of this book. Both the book and its author are better for her having done so.

Notes

Introduction

1. Traditionally by form we've indicated what Samuel Otter describes as the "relation of parts to wholes and inside to out." This is the form that dates back to the theories of the eighteenth-century German philosopher Immanuel Kant, whose influential *Critique of Judgment* (1790) established a "disinterested" mindset of perception according to which the sole focus for the viewer of an object (a painting, say, or a natural prospect) was restricted to the object in and of itself. Samuel Otter, "An Aesthetics in All Things," *Representations* 104 (Fall 2008): 119–20. For a timely defense of an expanded conception of formalism, see Christopher Castiglia and Russ Castronovo, "Preface: A 'Hive of Subtlety': Aesthetics and the End(s) of Cultural Studies," *American Literature* 76, no. 3 (September 2004): 424, 426–27; Jonathan Loesberg, *A Return to Aesthetics* (Stanford, CA: Stanford University Press, 2005), 9–13, 74–75, 98; and Isobel Armstrong, *The Radical Aesthetic* (Oxford: Wiley-Blackwell, 2000), 2–3, 38–39.

2. Kevin Lynch, *The Image of the City* (Cambridge, MA: MIT Press, 1960), 1–6, 46–48, 91.

3. In *Postmodern Urbanism* (Oxford: Blackwell, 1996), Nan
Ellin describes an outright "obsession with the text metaphor
for the city and culture" among enthusiasts of urban writing
and proponents of urban living (253). Interest in "city reading"
has since remained strong in the wake of David Henkin's
field-defining *City Reading: Written Words and Public Spaces
in Antebellum New York* (New York: Columbia University Press,
1998).

4. David Harvey, *Social Justice and the City* (1973; repr.
Athens: University of Georgia Press, 2008), 304.

5. Edward W. Soja, *Seeking Spatial Justice* (Minneapolis:
University of Minnesota Press, 2010), 70. In an earlier work,
Soja characterizes the conventional reliance within the
discipline of urban studies on the social and the historical as an
"interpretive dualism." Edward W. Soja, *Thirdspace: Journeys
to Los Angeles and Other Real-and-Imagined Places* (Oxford:
Blackwell, 1996), 5.

6. Nicholas Daly, *The Demographic Imagination and the
Nineteenth-Century City: Paris, London, New York* (Cambridge:
Cambridge University Press, 2015), 1, 11.

7. Caroline Levine, *Forms: Whole, Rhythm, Hierarchy,
Network* (Princeton, NJ: Princeton University Press, 2015), xi–xiii.

8. Speaking from the other side of form's recent revival in
our own century, Ellen Rooney contends that the "terror" of the
interpretive present is "the terror of formlessness." Ellen Rooney,
"Form and Contentment," *Modern Language Quarterly* 61, no. 1
(March 2000): 24.

9. Michel de Certeau, "Walking in the City," in *The Practice
of Everyday Life*, trans. Steven Randall (Berkeley: University of
California Press, 1984), 91–110.

10. Susan J. Wolfson, "Reading for Form," *Modern Language
Quarterly* 61, no. 1 (March 2000): 9, 7.

11. Hana Wirth-Neshner, "Impartial Maps: Reading and
Writing Cities," in *Handbook of Urban Studies*, ed. Ronan
Paddison (London: Sage, 2001), 54.

12. The German philosopher Hans-Georg Gadamer
maintains that such "prejudices" as we bring to bear on our

interpretations "are not necessarily unjustified and erroneous, so that they inevitably distort the truth." Rather, "prejudices are biases of our openness to the world," whereby "what we encounter says something to us." Hans-Georg Gadamer, *Philosophical Hermeneutics*, trans. and ed. David E. Linge (Berkeley: University of California Press, 1976), 9. Nicholas Daly, in his survey of the readable signage in the nineteenth-century city — a "discontinuous flotsam and jetsam of urban print," in his estimation — says that "city reading" is "a misleading term, in that it suggests a level of leisure and textual mastery that could barely have been possible" amid what he describes as a "frenzy of the legible" (*The Demographic Imagination*, 109). Peter Stallybrass, finally, argues that, beginning as early as the fifteenth century, the print form of the bound book (as opposed to the traditional scroll) allowed for a productive back-and-forth reading practice of "discontinuity." Peter Stallybrass, "Book and Scrolls: Navigating the Bible," in *Books and Readers in Early Modern England*, ed. Jennifer Andersen and Elizabeth Sauer (Philadelphia: University of Pennsylvania Press, 2002), 46, 73.

13. Henri Lefebvre, *The Production of Space*, trans. Donald Nicholson-Smith (Oxford: Blackwell, 1991), 81.

14. Laure Katsaros, *New York–Paris: Whitman, Baudelaire, and the Hybrid City* (Ann Arbor: University of Michigan Press, 2012), 1, 5.

15. Harold Bloom, *A Map of Misreading* (1975; repr. New York: Oxford University Press, 2003), xvi, 3–4, 9, 12. For a discussion of Bloom's work in its critical context, see Frank Lentricchia, *After the New Criticism* (Chicago: University of Chicago Press, 1981), 335–38.

1. Strong Reading, or the Literary Conversion of the Urban

1. Strong made these remarks upon reading Thomas Carlyle's German-inflected metaphysical novel *Sartor Resartus* (1836). See Strong's diary (hereafter *DGTS*), from *Diary of George Templeton Strong: Selections, 1835–1875*, 4 vols., ed. Allan Nevins and Milton Halsey Thomas (New York: Macmillan, 1952), 1:132.

2. Andreas Huyssen, *Present Pasts: Urban Palimpsests and the*

Politics of History (Stanford, CA: Stanford University Press, 2003), 1, 4.

3. Edwin Burrows and Mike Wallace, *Gotham: A History of New York to 1898* (New York: Oxford University Press, 1998), xvi.

4. According to David Scobey, "We cannot understand the making of the New York landscape . . . if we do not see it as a site of class negotiation and class struggle." Leading this "negotiation" were city readers like George Templeton Strong, men of property and social standing who left their imprint on the city as they "bought land, put up buildings, laid out parks, opened streets, and lent and borrowed capital in concert with and struggle against other class constituencies." David M. Scobey, *Empire City: The Making and Meaning of the New York City Landscape* (Philadelphia: Temple University Press, 2002), 35–36.

5. John F. Kasson, "The Semiotics of City-Living," in *Rudeness and Civility: Manners in Nineteenth-Century Urban America* (New York: Hill and Wang, 1990), 70; Hans Bergmann, *God in the Street: New York Writing from the Penny Press to Melville* (Philadelphia: Temple University Press, 1995), 10–11; and Michel Foucault, *The Order of Things: An Archaeology of the Human Sciences* (1966; repr. New York: Vintage, 1973), 53.

6. Edwin Hubbell Chapin, *Humanity in the City* (New York: DeWitt & Davenport, 1854), 10–11; Moritz Busch, *Travels between the Hudson and the Mississippi, 1851–1852*, ed. and trans. Norman Binger (Lexington: University of Kentucky Press, 1971), 33–34; and Isaac Lyon, *Recollections of an Old Cartman* (1872; repr. New York: New York Bound, 1984), 4–5.

7. Carl Smith, in his study *Urban Disorder and the Shape of Belief* (Chicago: University of Chicago Press, 1995), 10–11, contends that language, "as a system of figures and forms that convey meaning, is itself based on a concept of order, and is . . . summoned in moments of perceived crisis to stabilize and reassure the imagination, or at least to explain things in familiar terms."

8. Smith, *Urban Disorder*, 7.

9. In the order of their appearance, see the following: the

inaugural "manifesto" from *Arcturus*, in Perry Miller, *The Raven and the Whale* (New York: Harcourt, Brace & World, 1956), 90; the March 1844 issue of the *Expositor and Universalist Review*, from Cheryl D. Bohde, "'Magazines as a Powerful Element of Civilization': An Exploration of the Ideology of Literary Magazines, 1830–1859," *American Periodicals* 1 (1991): 38; Leroi M. Lee, "The Shoemaker of St. Austell," *Sartain's Union Magazine of Literature and Art*, July 1851, 353; Isaac Lyon, *Recollections*, 101–2; and Asa Greene, *A Glance at New York* (New York: A. Greene, 1837), 150. Refer as well to William H. Gilmore, *Reading Becomes a Necessity of Life: Material Cultural Life in Rural New England, 1780–1835* (Knoxville: University of Tennessee Press, 1992).

10. David Henkin, *City Reading: Written Words and Public Spaces in Antebellum New York* (New York: Columbia University Press, 1998), 28–31, 34.

11. Strong's mother, Eliza Catherine Templeton, was the second wife of Strong's father, his first having died at the age of twenty-nine.

12. The biographical background on Strong that appears here comes from *DGTS* I: xvi–xvii.

13. Strong took pride in his valuation of book prices and speaks often of his ability to purchase "very good old texts," his favorite phrase (*DGTS* I, 24: June 11, 1836).

14. Columbia College was one of the original subscribers to the formidable folio edition of Audubon's masterwork, paying $800 for a completed copy when the author/artist visited campus in 1833.

15. *Catalogue of the Books, Manuscripts, etc., of the Late George T. Strong, Esq.* (New York: C. C. Shelley, 1878).

16. James Wynne, *Private Libraries of New York* (New York: E. French, 1860), v, 377.

17. Additional titles from Strong's collection, not listed here, also fall into this same organizing vein. Some of these include Louis Aggasiz, *An Essay on Classification* (1849); François Arago, *Popular Astronomy* (1855); *The Works of Francis Bacon* (1740);

and, with implications for the "spectatorial" urban observer, *British Essayists. The Spectator, the Tatler, the Guardian, the Rambler, the Idler, etc.* (1842–1850).

18. Longfellow's poem may be read in its original publication context in the *Southern Literary Messenger*, November 1839, 709.

19. Strong refers here to the Five Points and Corlear's Hook, two Lower Manhattan neighborhoods associated in the nineteenth century with working- and criminal-class cultures.

20. Most notable among De Voe's acquisitions was his prized alphabetical listing (in five hundred folio pages of tidily written manuscript) of New York's earliest butchers, which sold at auction in April 1896 for twenty dollars. This was not long after the much mourned civic leader's death.

21. For an historical overview of critical writings on the image of the modern city, refer to Mary Ann Caws, ed., *City Images: Perspectives from Literature, Philosophy, and Film* (1991; repr. New York: Routledge, 2013).

22. Thomas Farrington De Voe, *Historical Incidents from Newspapers, 1800–1850*, 2:131. See Henkin, *City Reading*, 114–25, for a convincing spatial reading of the city daily. Carolyn Porter would deny that De Voe or any other "bourgeois man" was capable of "apprehending" the "objectified world" at all, "except in reified forms." Carolyn Porter, *Seeing and Being: The Plight of the Participant Observer in Emerson, James, Adams, and Faulkner* (Middletown, CT: Wesleyan University Press, 1981), 30.

23. Adam Tuchinsky, *Horace Greeley's* New-York Tribune: *Civil War–Era Socialism and the Crisis of Free Labor* (Ithaca, NY: Cornell University Press, 2009), 166.

24. This was particularly true in the print industry, which early on achieved sizable economies of scale before the Civil War through intensive regimens of mechanization.

25. On the cultures of labor in antebellum Manhattan, see Diane Lindstrom, "Economic Structure, Demographic Change, and Income Inequality in Antebellum New York," in *Power, Culture, and Place: Essays on New York City*, ed. John Hull Mollenkopf (New York: Russell Sage Foundation, 1988): 3–23; and Richard Stott, *Workers in the Metropolis: Class, Ethnicity,*

and Youth in Antebellum New York City (Ithaca, NY: Cornell University Press, 1990). The citation on "work" comes from James Dawson Burn, *Three Years among the Working-Classes* (London: Smith, Elder and Co., 1865), 11.

26. Abram C. Dayton, *Last Days of Knickerbocker Life in New York* (1882; repr. New York: G. P. Putnam's Sons, 1897), 147.

27. Horace Greeley, "Coming to the City" (1850), from *Hints toward Reforms, in Lectures, Addresses, and Other Writings* (New York: Fowlers and Wells, 1855), 360.

28. Two studies emphasize the chronic indirection of period laborers' protests: Sean Wilentz, *Chants Democratic: New York City and the Rise of the American Working Class, 1788–1850* (New York: Oxford University Press, 1984); and Eric Lott, *Love and Theft: Blackface Minstrelsy and the American Working Class* (New York: Oxford University Press, 1995).

29. Raymond Williams, *Keywords: A Vocabulary of Culture and Society* (New York: Oxford University Press, 1985), 60–69; Sharon Cameron, *Thinking in Henry James* (Chicago: University of Chicago Press, 1991), 6–7, 29.

30. Michael C. Cohen, *The Social Lives of Poems in Nineteenth-Century America* (Philadelphia: University of Pennsylvania Press, 2015), 18–19; Catherine Robson, *Heart Beats: Everyday Life and the Memorized Poem* (Princeton, NJ: Princeton University Press, 2012), 10–11.

31. Robert Darnton, *The Great Cat Massacre and Other Episodes in French Cultural History* (New York: Basic Books, 1984), 227. The reader Darnton has in mind is Jean-Jacques Rousseau, who he says "never learned to distinguish between literature and reality." Steven Knapp explores a general fixation with letters in *Literary Interest: The Limits of Anti-Formalism* (Cambridge, MA: Harvard University Press, 1993), 49–50. Kant's *Critique of Reason* (1781; trans. 1838) appears as listing no. 915 in the Strong *Catalogue*. The philosopher's distinction between the "Beautiful" ("connected with the form of the object") and the "Sublime" ("to be found in the formless object") appears in the third of his "critiques," *The Critique of Judgement*, trans. J. H. Bernard (1790; repr. London: MacMillan, 1914), 101–2. The

citation from *Arcturus* appears in "The Wants of Man," October 1841, 312.

2. Reading the Urban Form of Fire

1. Carl Smith, *Urban Disorder and the Shape of Belief* (Chicago: University of Chicago Press, 1995).

2. Benjamin, in a letter from March 1931 to Max Rychner, *The Correspondence of Walter Benjamin*, trans. M. R. and E. M. Jacobson (Chicago: University of Chicago Press, 1994), 371–73.

3. Ignacio Farías, "Introduction: Decentering the Object of Urban Studies," in *Urban Assemblages: How Actor-Network Theory Changes Urban Studies*, ed. Ignacio Farías and Thomas Bender (New York: Routledge, 2010), 1–2.

4. My statistics on New York's antebellum fires are from Henkin, *City Reading*, 34. Also see Junius Henri Browne, *The Great Metropolis: A Mirror of New York* (Hartford, CT: American Publishing Company, 1869), 565.

5. Margaret Hindle Hazen and Robert M. Hazen, *Keepers of the Flame: The Role of Fire in American Culture, 1775–1925* (Princeton, NJ: Princeton University Press, 1992), 8.

6. Smith, *Urban Disorder*, 3.

7. Gaston Bachelard, *On Poetic Imagination and Reverie*, trans. Collette Gaudin (1971; repr. Putnam, CT: Spring, 2005), 2.

8. Salomon de Rothschild, December 17, 1859, in *A Casual View of America: The Home Letters of Salomon de Rothschild, 1859–1861*, ed. Sigmund Diamond (Stanford, CA: Stanford University Press, 1961), 17. Refer as well to David M. Stewart, *Reading and Disorder in Antebellum America* (Columbus: Ohio State University Press, 2011), 89.

9. Leah Price, *How to Do Things with Books in Victorian Britain* (Princeton, NJ: Princeton University Press, 2012), 2; Lewis Mumford, *The City in History: Its Origins, Its Transformations, Its Prospects* (New York: Harcourt, Brace, and World, 1961), 99.

10. Henkin, *City Reading*, 35.

11. Keeping with her biblical theme, Child recounts "heat like that of the furnace which tried Shadrach, Meschach, and

Abednego." Lydia Maria Child, April 7, 1842, in *Letters from New-York*, ed. Bruce Mills (Athens: University of Georgia Press, 1998), 70.

12. "AWFUL CALAMITY," *New York Sun*, Friday morning, December 18, 1835, 2.

13. J. Frank Kernan, *Reminiscences of the Old Fire Laddies and Volunteer Fire Departments of New York and Brooklyn, Together with a Complete History of the Paid Departments of Both Cities* (New York: M. Crane, 1885), 186–87.

14. Ash Amin and Nigel Thrift, *Cities: Reimagining the Urban* (Cambridge: Polity, 2002), 8–9. "Transitivity" is the authors' name for the "openness" they describe, which they attribute equally to the city's spatial and temporal dimensions.

15. Amin and Thrift, *Cities*, 93–104. The authors' phrase for the modern city's management of complex bodily encounters is "the engineering of certainty."

16. In *Chants Democratic*, 259–63, Sean Wilentz describes the rowdy physical culture of volunteer firemen in antebellum New York. Bruce Laurie does the same for the early fire companies of Philadelphia in *Working People of Philadelphia, 1800–1850* (Philadelphia: Temple University Press, 1980), 71–77. Both historians stress the vigorous nature of working-class firemen's labors.

17. Herbert Asbury, *Ye Olde Fire Laddies* (New York: Knopf, 1930), 85; Kernan, quoting his friend Michael Crane, in *Reminiscences*, 25.

18. Amy Greenberg, *Cause for Alarm: The Volunteer Fire Department in the Nineteenth-Century City* (Princeton, NJ: Princeton University Press, 1998), 9, 85. The *New-York Tribune* contributor Asa Greene offered a similar reading of fire companies' class composition for nineteenth-century New York. He writes, "The fire companies are composed of young men mostly between the ages of twenty and thirty. They are clerks and mechanics; but a majority of the latter." Asa Greene, *A Glance at New York* (New York: A. Greene, 1837), 209.

19. Abram C. Dayton, *Last Days of Knickerbocker Life in New York* (1882; repr. New York: G. P. Putnam's Sons, 1897), 163.

Before the city's sharp northward expansion at midcentury, New York in the spring of 1835 made the bell atop its City Hall into a central signifying system for the inhabitants of Lower Manhattan. In the event of a fire, the number and sequence of bells tolled served to indicate the municipal precinct in which a blaze had started, thereby directing volunteer companies in their response. Once the city was too large to be walkable and its separate neighborhoods too scattered for a single bell to be audible, authorities ceased to rely on City Hall as a central fire signal. In time the Common Council authorized the construction of permanent signaling stations throughout the city, many of these attached to the cupolas of such area landmarks as markets, reservoirs, and the Halls of Justice, or Tombs Prison.

20. Alvin F. Harlow, *Old Bowery Days: The Chronicles of a Famous Street* (New York: D. Appleton: 1931), 202.

21. Asbury, *Ye Olde Fire Laddies*, 140.

22. A. E. Costello, *Birth of the Bravest: A History of the New York Fire Department from 1609 to 1887* (1887; repr. New York: Tom Doherty Associates, 2002), 159.

23. Elliot Gorn, "'Good-Bye Boys, I Die a True American': Homicide, Nativism, and Working-Class Culture in Antebellum New York City," *Journal of American History* 74, no. 2 (1987): 408. The "action" and "adventure" mentioned by Gorn set firemen in opposition to the "formality and restraint" that, Karen Halttunen claims, in these years "grew increasingly important as markers of status among urban Americans of the emerging middle class." Decorum was "anathema to firemen," Halttunen says. At least one contemporary fireman agreed. "Formality is but another name for restraint of body and mind," he wrote in the *California Spirit of the Times and Fireman's Journal* (November 19, 1859), "and that is a fireman's pet horror." This last and Halttunen's statements are from Karen Halttunen, *Confidence Men and Painted Women: A Study of Middle-Class Culture in America* (New Haven, CT: Yale University Press, 1982), 59.

24. Greenberg, *Cause for Alarm*, 6.

25. Kasson, *Rudeness and Civility*, 124.

26. Costello, *Birth of the Bravest*, 253; *New York Sun*, Friday morning, December 18, 1835, 2.

27. Dayton, *Last Days*, 163.

28. John Fanning Watson makes these characterizations of volunteer firemen in his *Annals of Philadelphia and Pennsylvania, in the Olden Time* (Philadelphia: John Penington and Uriah Hunt, 1844), 498.

29. Asbury, *Ye Olde Fire Laddies*, 184–85.

30. By 1866, fifteen American cities had switched from manual to steam power for their fire engines. Ten years later, the number had risen to 275 municipal fire departments using steam. These last, as many of them said, had enlisted "fire to fight fire." This switch was hardly immediate and wholesale in the rest of the country, however. Cultural resistance as much as a lack of adequate financial resources meant that the volunteer system persisted in smaller towns of the United States well into the twentieth century. For more on this transition, see Hazen and Hazen, *Keepers of the Flame*, 123–29.

31. Browne, *The Great Metropolis*, 564, 567.

32. Dayton, *Last Days*, 163; Harlow, *Old Bowery Days*, 203; Asbury, *Ye Olde Fire Laddies*, 84; Kernan, *Reminiscences*, 26.

33. On one memorable occasion, in 1861, at a fire at Houston and the Bowery, the volunteer Jim Hurley, from New York's Forest Company No. 3, reportedly held thousands of listeners enthralled by his rendition of the old Irish ballad "Shula Agra." Harlow, *Old Bowery Days*, 203.

34. Greenberg, *Cause for Alarm*, 39.

35. Costello, *Birth of the Bravest*, 155–58.

36. Nathaniel Currier, one half of the popular-print producers Currier and Ives, was himself a volunteer fireman in New York in the 1850s.

3. The Revolutionary Formalism of France

1. Henri Lefebvre, *The Production of Space*, trans. Donald Nicholson-Smith (Oxford: Blackwell, 1991), 16.

2. Caroline Levine, *Forms: Whole, Rhythm, Hierarchy, Network* (Princeton, NJ: Princeton University Press, 2015), 2.

3. Charles Eliot Norton, *Letters of Charles Eliot Norton*, ed. Sara Norton and M. A. De Wolfe Howe (Boston: Houghton, Mifflin, 1913), 1:446.

4. Adam Tuchinsky, *Horace Greeley's* New-York Tribune: *Civil War–Era Socialism and the Crisis of Free Labor* (Ithaca, NY: Cornell University Press, 2009), 84–85.

5. Asa Greene, *A Glance at New York* (New York: A. Greene, 1837), 95–96.

6. N. P. Willis, Letter I (March 1832) and Letter XI (May 1834), in *Pencillings by the Way* (London: George Virtue, 1842), 1–2, 345–46.

7. Vanessa Schwartz, *Spectacular Realities: Early Mass Culture in Fin-de-Siècle Paris* (Berkeley: University of California Press, 1998), 6.

8. Fuller stayed in Paris from November 13, 1846, to February 25, 1847. Her itinerary included an extended stay in London beforehand and Rome, famously, afterward. Most of her commentary discussed here comes from her *Tribune* column, "Things and Thoughts in Europe." Cited here, respectively, are passages from Letters no. XI (March 31, 1847), no. XII (May 15, 1847), no. X (March 3, 1847), and no. XIII (May 29, 1847). These appear in Margaret Fuller, *"These Sad but Glorious Days": Dispatches from Europe, 1846–1850*, ed. Larry J. Reynolds and Susan Belasco Smith (New Haven, CT: Yale University Press, 1991), 113, 119, 108, 120, 126. The recipient of Fuller's private correspondence was her friend Mary Roth, from *The Letters of Margaret Fuller*, ed. Robert Hudspeth (Ithaca, NY: Cornell University Press, 1987), 4:273 (May 1847).

9. Fuller, Letter no. XI, "Things and Thoughts in Europe," 113–14.

10. Larry J. Reynolds, *European Revolutions and the American Literary Renaissance* (New Haven, CT: Yale University Press, 1988), 60–61.

11. Fuller, Letter no. XII, "Things and Thoughts in Europe," 123, 119.

12. Reynolds, *European Revolutions*, 3.

13. "The formal institutions overthrown or founded by a revolution are easily discernible, but they do not measure its effects." Eric Hobsbawm, *The Age of Revolution: Europe, 1789–1848* (London: Abacus, 1977), 182.

14. Of the nine hundred available seats in France's Constituent Assembly, radicals would win only one hundred.

15. Historians disagree over the demographics of the men and women who joined the insurgency in June. Of special interest are the respective contributions and composition of France's middle and working classes. See Roger Magraw, *A History of the French Working Class, vol. 1: The Age of Artisan Revolution, 1815–1871* (Cambridge, MA: Blackwell, 1992), 3; T. J. Clark, *The Absolute Bourgeois: Artists and Politics in France, 1848–1851* (Berkeley: University of California Press, 1999), 9–10; and Roger Price, *The French Second Republic: A Social History* (Ithaca, NY: Cornell University Press, 1972), 5–7, 162–78.

16. Clark, *The Absolute Bourgeois*, 9–10.

17. Alexis de Tocqueville, *The Recollections of Alexis de Tocqueville*, trans. Alexander Teixeira de Mattos (London: Harvill, 1948), 12–13. Tocqueville made these remarks on January 29, 1848.

18. Reynolds, *European Revolutions*, 4.

19. Priscilla Ferguson, *Paris as Revolution: Writing the Nineteenth-Century City* (Berkeley: University of California Press, 1994), 1.

20. This estimate is from Reynolds, *European Revolutions*, 45.

21. New York *Courier and Enquirer*, July 14, 1848, 1.

22. Samuel Goodrich, *Recollections of a Lifetime; or, Men and Things I Have Seen* (New York: Arundel, 1856), 828–30. Goodrich would serve as U.S. consul at Paris from 1851 to 1853.

23. Charles A. Dana, dispatch from Paris, *New-York Tribune*, July 14, 1848, 2. The dateline for Dana's report is June 29.

24. Although less moderate than most, Karl Marx ironically wrote not long after the June Days had ended that "the February Revolution was the beautiful revolution." Here the inveterate revolutionary carefully chooses a language of sensory gratification to (over)compensate for the profound political disappointments

that readers like him had come to experience in the aftermath of all that had happened in Paris. See Karl Marx, from the *Neue Rheinische Zeitung*, June 29, 1848, cited in Clark, *Absolute Bourgeois*, 9. Note that Marx launched the daily *Neue Rheinische Zeitung* in Cologne, Germany, in 1848, during one of his several exiles in those years from Paris.

25. Beginning in 1847, Mitchell apprenticed at law in the Wall Street office of John Osborne Sargent, described by the *New York Times* upon his death in 1891 as "one of the most noted lawyers of the last fifty years." For more on Sargent, see his obituary in the *New York Times,* December 29, 1891; and also Waldo Hillary Dunn, *The Life of Donald G. Mitchell, Ik Marvel* (New York: Charles Scribner's Sons, 1922), 178–79.

26. Donald Grant Mitchell [Ik. Marvel], *The Battle Summer: Being Transcripts from Personal Observation in Paris, during the Year 1848* (New York: Baker & Scribner, 1850), ii–iii. The date for the volume's dedicatory letter reads New York, November 1849.

27. Clark, *The Absolute Bourgeois*, 16, observes that the Paris barricades became the ultimate "disputed symbol" of revolutionary Paris because they were read differently by different classes.

28. Warren Magnusson, *Politics of Urbanism: Seeing Like a City* (New York: Routledge, 2011), 35, 111–18.

29. Richard Sennett, "'The Social Question': Reformers in Paris Explore a Puzzle," in *Together: The Rituals, Pleasures, and Politics of Cooperation* (New Haven, CT: Yale University Press, 2012), 37.

4. Photography and the Image of the City

1. Shawn Michelle Smith, *At the Edge of Sight: Photography and the Unseen* (Durham, NC: Duke University Press, 2013), 4, 8. Also see Jonathan Crary, *Techniques of the Observer: On Vision and Modernity in the Nineteenth Century* (Cambridge, MA: MIT Press, 1990), 1–24. On the "textuality" of the visual arts generally, see James A. W. Heffernan, "Reading Pictures," *PMLA* 134, no. 1 (January 2019): 18–34.

2. F. O. Matthiessen, *American Renaissance: Art and Expression in the Age of Emerson and Whitman* (New York: Oxford University Press, 1941), 51.

3. Ben Yagoda, *About Town:* The New Yorker *and the World It Made* (New York: Da Capo, 2001), 12, 59. The city readers of Yagoda's discussion include the writers, editors, and readers of the *New Yorker* magazine upon its founding, in 1925.

4. Elisa Tamarkin, "Losing Perspective in the Age of News," *PMLA* 125, no. 1 (January 2010): 199.

5. Luc Sante, *Low Life: Lures and Snares of Old New York* (New York: Vintage, 1992), 301–3.

6. W. J. T. Mitchell, *Iconology: Image, Text, Ideology* (Chicago: University of Chicago Press, 1986), 160, 164, 167, 173. Without ever defining "image" as such, Mitchell does provide what he terms a "genealogy" of image "types," which runs from "graphic," "optical," and "perceptual" at one end of the visual spectrum to "mental" and "verbal" at the other (9–10).

7. Alan Trachtenberg, *Reading American Photographs: Images as History* (New York: Hill and Wang, 1989), 3.

8. As Marcy Dinius reminds us, most people first encountered the "new imaging medium" of the daguerreotype "through written descriptions . . . that were published and rapidly reprinted throughout the country." The upshot of this "encounter" is that the mass of Americans assimilated this visual revolution verbally, in a secondhand way. Marcy J. Dinius, *The Camera and the Press: American Visual and Print Culture in the Age of the Daguerreotype* (Philadelphia: University of Pennsylvania Press, 2012), 1–3.

9. One year earlier, in 1837, Daguerre recorded an indoor image of his studio, reputed to be the first completely successful example of his process.

10. Samuel Morse's remarks appeared in a letter he wrote to his brothers, both newspaper editors. They in turn published Morse's response, which ranks among the first commentaries by an American on the new medium, in the *New-York Observer* on April 20, 1839. Morse's original letter is reprinted in Helmut Gernsheim and Alison Gernsheim, *L. J. M. Daguerre: The*

History of the Diorama and the Daguerreotype, 2nd ed. (New York: Dover, 1968), 89–90.

11. Lutz Koepnick, "Reading on the Move," *PMLA* 128, no. 1 (January 2013): 232–33.

12. In our own digital age, David Mikics says that "reading better means reading more slowly." David Mikics, *Slow Reading in a Hurried Age* (Cambridge, MA: Harvard University Press, 2013), 1.

13. Not until the introduction, in 1855, of a new paper-based photographic process was it possible to reproduce in print any images made from this same medium. Until that time, any such image would have been reproduced indirectly, in some approximate form of etching, engraving, or lithograph. The image shown here, one of two that Thiébault produced within the embattled span of four days, ran subsequently inside a special August issue of the magazine *Journées Illustrées de la Révolution de 1848*.

14. "Daguerreotyping in New York," *Daguerreian Journal*, November 15, 1850, 49.

15. This *Journal* report appeared in July 1839, as cited in Floyd Rinhart and Marion Rinhart, *The American Daguerreotype* (Athens: University of Georgia Press, 1981), 15.

16. British sources had already made English translations available in America, before U.S. translators went to work. Not all of these initial translations were derived straight from Daguerre. François Arago summarized the daguerreotype process in a speech before the French Academy of Sciences in Paris on January 7, 1839, before Daguerre's report. His was the first such announcement anywhere (and in any language) of what would soon be known as photography. It was this same source, Arago, from whom a number of readers in England and the United States learned of the vaunted "process."

17. "The New Art," New York *Morning Herald* (September 30, 1839), as cited in Rinhart and Rinhart, *American Daguerreotype*, 25–26.

18. Alan Trachtenberg, "Photography: The Emergence of a

Keyword," in *Photography in Nineteenth-Century America*, ed.
Martha A Sandweiss (Fort Worth, TX: Amon Carter Museum;
New York: Abrams, 1991), 17, 20; Rinhart and Rinhart, *American
Daguerreotype*, 95; Beaumont Newhall, *The Daguerreotype in
America*, 3rd ed. (New York: Dover 1976), 34.

19. "Editor's Table: The 'Daguerreotype,'" *Knickerbocker*,
December 1839, 560–61.

20. "The Daguerreotype," *New-Yorker*, December 14, 1839,
205. The comments from the *Observer* appear in Dinius, *Camera
and the Press*, 25.

21. H. H. Snelling, "The Art of Photography," *Photographic
Art Journal*, January 1851, 1–3.

22. "Something about Pictures," *Atlantic Monthly*, February
1858, 402.

23. Peter B. Hales, *Silver Cities: The Photography of American
Urbanization, 1839–1915* (Philadelphia: Temple University Press,
1984), 17.

24. Hales, *Silver Cities*, 2–4, 7, 15.

25. There is no surviving correspondence either to or from
Prevost, which means that our "readings" of his work must
be based largely on the visual evidence at hand. For more on
Prevost's place in the history of photography, see Julie Mellby,
"Victor Prevost: Painter, Lithographer, Photographer," *History of
Photography* 35, no. 3 (2011): 221–39.

26. Hales, *Silver Cities*, 17.

27. Some sixty of Prevost's New York photographs survive.
The New-York Historical Society holds forty-two of these. The
Museum of the City of New York, Prints and Photographs
Collection, holds the rest. Prevost's rare comments come from a
published letter he wrote to the editor of the *Photographic and
Fine Art Journal* 7, no. 9 (September 1854): 287.

28. Hales, *Silver Cities*, 72.

29. For one example of the urban-view book, see the
English-born Californian G. R. Fardon's *San Francisco Album:
Photographs of the Most Beautiful Views and Public Buildings of
San Francisco* (1856).

30. David Brewster, *The Stereoscope; Its History, Theory, and Construction, with Its Application to the Fine and Useful Arts and Education* (London: John Murray, 1856), 193.

31. Hales, *Silver Cities*, 87.

32. Oliver Wendell Holmes, "Sun-Painting and Sun-Sculpture; with a Stereoscopic Trip across the Atlantic," *Atlantic Monthly*, July 1861, 17–18.

33. Hales, *Silver Cities*, 87.

34. Oliver Wendell Holmes, "The Stereoscope and the Stereograph," *Atlantic Monthly*, June 1859, 738; Holmes, "Sun-Painting and Sun-Sculpture," 15–16.

35. Holmes, "Sun-Painting and Sun-Sculpture," 17–18.

36. H., "The Daguerreotype," *Bulletin of the American Art-Union*, November 1850, 131; Herman Melville, "Inscription Epistolary," in *John Marr and Other Sailors* (1888), from *The Works of Herman Melville* (London: Constable and Co., 1924), 194.

Afterword

1. "City of Print: New York and the Periodical Press," http://cityofprint.net.

2. "Mapping the Bookstore: Retail Cartographies in Antebellum Manhattan," Columbia Book History Colloquium, March 25, 2014.

3. New York Scapes, http://newyorkscapes.org.

4. Nicolas Bourriaud, *Relational Aesthetics*, trans. Simon Pleasance and Fronza Woods (Dijon, France: Les presses du réel, 2002), 11, 13.

Bibliography

Periodicals

Arcturus, A Journal of Books and Opinions
    D. [Duyckinck, Evert A.]. "Newspapers" (January 1841): 69.
    "The Wants of Man" (October 1841): 310–13.
    Mathews, Cornelius. "A Movement in Clerkdom" (November
        1841): 337–41.
    "Magazine Literature" (November 1841): 342–44.
    "The City Book-Stalls" (November 1841): 345–50.
Atlantic Monthly
    Holmes, Oliver Wendell. "The Stereoscope and the
        Stereograph" (June 1859): 738–48.
    ———. "Sun-Painting and Sun-Sculpture; with a Stereoscopic
        Trip across the Atlantic" (July 1861): 13–30.
    O'Brien, Fitz-James. "The Diamond Lens" (January 1858):
        354–67.
    "The Representative Art" (June 1860): 687–93.
    "Something about Pictures" (February 1858): 402–10.
Bulletin of the American Art-Union
    H. "The Daguerreotype" (November 1850): 131–32.
Commercial Advertiser (1830–1840)

Court and Lady's Magazine, Monthly Critic and Museum
    (London)
    Janin, Jules. "La Daguerreotype" (October 1839): 436–39.
Daguerreian Journal
    "Daguerreotyping in New York" (November 15, 1850): 49–50.
Frank Leslie's Popular Monthly
    "Grand Demonstration of Workingmen" (September 16,
        1882): 53.
Harper's Monthly Magazine
    Brewster, David. "Obstructions to the Use of the Telescope"
        (October 1850): 699–701.
    "Fashions for Early Summer" (June 1850): 142–44.
    "The Inconstant Daguerreotype" (May 1855): 820–26.
    "Michelet, the French Historian" (Feb. 1851): 353–56.
    "The Paris Election" (June 1850): 116.
    "A Paris Newspaper" (July 1850): 181–83.
The Horticulturist: Journal of Rural Art and Rural Taste
    [Downing, Andrew Jackson]. "A Talk about Public Parks and
        Gardens" (October 1848): 153–58.
Knickerbocker
    [Clark, Lewis Gaylord]. "Editors' Table: The 'Daguerreotype'"
        (December 1839): 560–61.
La Mode (Paris)
    "Caricature of La Mode" (October 26, 1839): 106, with fold-
        out sheet.
New York Sun (morning edition, December 1835)
New-York Tribune (February–July 1848)
New-Yorker
    "The Daguerreotype" (December 14, 1839): 205.
The Photographic Art Journal
    [Snelling, H. H.]. "The Art of Photography" (January 1851):
        1–3.
The Photographic and Fine Art Journal
    Prevost, Victor. "Letter to the Editor" (September 1854): 287.
    Root, Marcus A. "A Trip to Boston — Boston Artists" (August
        1855): 246–47.

Putnam's Monthly Magazine
"Lawyers" (November 1856): 449–59.
"New-York Church Architecture" (Sept. 1853): 233–49.
"New York Daguerreotyped" (February 1853): 121–36.
"New York Daguerreotyped" (April 1853): 353–69.
"Sketches in a Parisian Café" (December 1853): 627–32.
Sartain's Union Magazine of Literature and Art
Kirkland, Caroline. "Streets of Paris — The Boulevard" (June 1851): 401–5.
Lee, Leroi M. "The Shoemaker of St. Austell" (July 1851): 348–55.
Scribner's Monthly Magazine
"How to See New York" (June 1876): 272–76.
Southern Literary Messenger
Longfellow, Henry Wadsworth. "The Beleaguered City" (November 1839): 709.

Primary Sources

Abdy, Edward S. *Journal of a Residence and Tour in the United States of North America, from April, 1833, to October, 1834.* London: John Murray, 1835.
Alison, Archibald. *Essays on the Nature and Principles of Taste.* 1790; repr. Edinburgh: Archibald Constable and Company, 1815.
Asbury, Herbert. *Ye Olde Fire Laddies.* New York: Knopf, 1930.
Atkinson, Edward. "Commercial Development." In *The First Century of the Republic: A Review of American Progress*, ed. Theodore Dwight Woolsey, 200–10. New York: Harper & Brothers, 1876.
Barnum, Phineas T. *Struggles and Triumphs; or, Forty Years' Recollections of P. T. Barnum.* 1869; repr. Buffalo: Warren, Johnson & Co., 1873.
Barton, H. Arnold, ed. *Letters from the Promised Land: Swedes in America, 1840–1914.* Minneapolis: University of Minnesota Press, 1975.

Baudelaire, Charles. *Les fleurs du mal* [1857]. Trans. Keith
  Waldrop. Middletown, CT: Wesleyan University Press, 2006.
———. "The Painter of Modern Life" (1859). In *The Painter of
  Modern Life and Other Essays*, ed. Jonathan Mayne, 1–41.
  London: Phaidon, 1995.
Beecher, Henry Ward. "Reading." In *Eyes and Ears*, 187–89.
  Boston: Ticknor and Fields, 1862.
Brace, Charles Loring. *The Dangerous Classes of New York, and
  Twenty Years' Work among Them.* New York: Wynkoop &
  Hallenbeck, 1872.
Brewster, David. *The Stereoscope; Its History, Theory, and
  Construction, with Its Application to the Fine and Useful Arts
  and Education.* London: John Murray, 1856.
Brisbane, Albert. *Association; or, A Concise Exposition of the
  Practical Part of Fourier's Social Science.* New York: Greeley
  and McElrath, 1843.
Browne, Junius Henri. *The Great Metropolis: A Mirror of New
  York.* Hartford, CT: American Publishing Company, 1869.
Burke, Edmund. *A Philosophical Enquiry into the Origin of Our
  Ideas of the Sublime and Beautiful.* 1757; London: J. Dodsley,
  1759.
Burn, James Dawson. *Three Years among the Working-Classes.*
  London: Smith, Elder and Co., 1865.
Busch, Moritz. *Travels between the Hudson and the Mississippi,
  1851–1852.* Ed. and trans. Norman Binger. Lexington:
  University of Kentucky Press, 1971.
Carlyle, Thomas. *Sartor Resartus.* 1836; repr. Boston: Athenaeum,
  1902.
*Catalogue of the Books, Manuscripts, etc., of the Late George T.
  Strong, Esq., Comprising Manuscripts, Missals, Psalters,
  etc., Richly Illuminated in Gold and Colors, Five Specimens
  of Early Printing, Rare, Curious and Standard Books, Early
  English Poetry and the Drama, Choice Editions of the Greek
  and the Latin Classics, etc., etc., Which Will be Sold at
  Auction, by Messrs. Bangs & Co., 656 Broadway, New York,
  Monday, November 4th, 1878, and Following Days. Sale to*

Begin Each Day Promptly at 3:30 *P.M.* New York: C. C.
   Shelley, 1878.

Chapin, Edwin Hubbell. *Humanity in the City.* New York:
   DeWitt & Davenport, 1854.

——. *Moral Aspects of City Life.* New York: Henry Lyon, 1853.

Child, Lydia Maria. *Letters from New-York.* 1st series, 1843. Ed.
   Bruce Mills. Athens: University of Georgia Press, 1998.

——. *Lydia Maria Child: Selected Letters, 1817–1880.* Ed.
   Milton Meltzer, Patricia G. Holland, and Francine Krasno.
   Amherst, MA: University of Massachusetts Press, 1982.

Costello, A. E. *Birth of the Bravest: A History of the New York
   Fire Department from 1609 to 1887.* 1887; repr. New York: Tom
   Doherty Associates, 2002.

Dayton, Abram C. *Last Days of Knickerbocker Life in New York.*
   1882; repr. New York: G. P. Putnam's Sons, 1897.

De Voe, Thomas Farrington. *Historical Incidents from
   Newspapers, 1800–1850.* Vol. 2. Manuscript Collection,
   New-York Historical Society.

Engels, Friedrich. *The Condition of the Working Class in
   England.* 1845; repr. New York: Penguin, 1987.

*Fire Marshal's Report, to the Mayor, Common Council and
   Police Justices of the City and County of New York.* New York:
   Chatterton & Brothers, June 1 to November 30, 1859.

Foster, George G. *New York by Gas-Light.* Ed. Stuart Blumin.
   1850; repr. Berkeley: University of California Press, 1990.

Fuller, Margaret. *Margaret Fuller, Critic: Writings from the
   New-York Tribune, 1844–1846.* Ed. Judith Mattson Bean and
   Joel Myerson. New York: Columbia University Press, 2000.

——. *"These Sad but Glorious Days": Dispatches from Europe,
   1846–1850.* Ed. Larry J. Reynolds and Susan Belasco Smith.
   New Haven, CT: Yale University Press, 1991.

——. *The Letters of Margaret Fuller.* Ed. Robert Hudspeth.
   Ithaca, NY: Cornell University Press, 1983.

Gilman and Mower. *The Photographer's Guide, in Which
   the Daguerrean Art Is Familiarly Explained.* Lowell, MA:
   Samuel O. Dearborn, 1842.

Goodrich, Samuel. *Recollections of a Lifetime; or, Men and Things I Have Seen*. New York: Arundel, 1856.

Greeley, Horace. *Hints toward Reforms, in Lectures, Addresses and Other Writings*. 1850; repr. New York: Fowlers and Wells, 1855.

Greene, Asa. *A Glance at New York*. New York: A. Greene, 1837.

Harlow, Alvin F. *Old Bowery Days: The Chronicles of a Famous Street*. New York: D. Appleton, 1931.

Hone, Philip. *The Diary of Philip Hone, 1828–1851*. Ed. Bayard Tuckerman. New York: Dodd, Mead and Co., 1889.

Jarves, James Jackson. *Art Thoughts: The Experiences and Observations of an American Amateur in Europe*. Boston: Houghton, Mifflin and Co., 1896.

———. *The Art-Idea: Sculpture, Painting, and Architecture in America*. New York: Hurd and Houghton, 1865.

Kant, Immanuel. *The Critique of Judgement* [1790]. Trans. J. H. Bernard. London: MacMillan and Co., 1914.

Kernan, J. Frank. *Reminiscences of the Old Fire Laddies and Volunteer Fire Departments of New York and Brooklyn, Together with a Complete History of the Paid Departments of Both Cities*. New York: M. Crane, 1885.

Kirkland, Frazar. *Cyclopaedia of Commercial and Business Anecdotes*. 2 vols. New York: D. Appleton, 1864.

Lyon, Isaac. *Recollections of an Old Cartman*. 1872; repr. New York: New York Bound, 1984.

Marryat, Frederick. *A Diary in America, with Remarks on Its Institutions*. Paris: A. and W. Galignani and Co., 1839.

Marx, Karl. *Dispatches for the* New-York Tribune: *Selected Journalism of Karl Marx*. Ed. James Ledbetter. New York: Penguin, 2007.

———. *The Eighteenth Brumaire of Louis Bonaparte* [1852]. In *Marx's Eighteenth Brumaire: (Post)modern Interpretations*, ed. Mark Cowling and James Martin, 19–109. London: Pluto, 2002.

Mathews, Cornelius. *A Pen-and-Ink Panorama of New York City*. New York: John S. Taylor, 1853.

Maverick, Augustus. *Henry J. Raymond and the New York Press*. Hartford, CT: A. S. Hale, 1870.

Melville, Herman. *The Writings of Herman Melville. Vol. 14: Correspondence*. Ed. Lynn Horth. Evanston, IL: Northwestern University Press and the Newberry Library, 1993.

———. *John Marr and Other Sailors* [1888]. In *The Works of Herman Melville*, 192–244. London: Constable and Co., 1924.

———. "Bartleby, the Scrivener: A Story of Wall Street" [1853]. In *The Writings of Herman Melville. Vol. 9: The Piazza Tales and Other Prose Pieces, 1839–1860*. Ed. Harrison Hayford, Hershel Parker, and G. Thomas Tanselle, 13–45. Evanston, IL: Northwestern University Press, 1987.

———. *The Writings of Herman Melville. Vol. 7: Pierre, or the Ambiguities* [1852]. Ed. Harrison Hayford, Hershel Parker, and G. Thomas Tanselle. Evanston, IL: Northwestern University Press and the Newberry Library, 1971.

Mitchell, Donald Grant [Ik. Marvel]. *The Battle Summer: Being Transcripts from Personal Observation in Paris, During the Year 1848*. New York: Baker & Scribner, 1850.

———. *The Lorgnette, or, Studies of the Town by an Opera-Goer*. New York: Stringer and Townsend, 1851.

Norton, Charles Eliot. *Letters of Charles Eliot Norton*. Ed. Sara Norton and M. A. De Wolfe Howe. Boston: Houghton, Mifflin and Co., 1913.

Olmsted, Frederick Law. *The Papers of Frederick Law Olmsted. Vol. 3: Creating Central Park, 1857–1861*. Ed. Charles Beveridge and David Schuyler. Baltimore, MD: Johns Hopkins University Press, 1983.

———. *Public Parks and the Enlargement of Towns: Read before the American Social Science Association at the Lowell Institute, Boston, Feb. 25, 1870*. Cambridge, MA: American Social Science Association, 1870.

Programme of the Scenery, Action and Tableaux: With Words of the Songs, Choruses, &c. of the Musical and Scenic Romance Called "The Enchanted Beauty! Or, The Dream of a Hundred Years." Being the fifth of the series of the Museum grand spectacles. Boston: W. Marden, 1850.

Robinson, H. R. *The Great Fire of the City of New York, 16 December 1835*. Published January 1836, by the proprietor H. R. Robinson.

Rothschild, Salomon de. *A Casual View of America: The Home
    Letters of Salomon de Rothschild, 1859–1861.* Ed. Sigmund
    Diamond. Stanford, CA: Stanford University Press, 1961.
Schiller, Friedrich. *On the Aesthetic Education of Man.* 1794;
    repr. Ithaca, NY: Cornell University Library, 2009.
Sewell, H. *Hanington's Dioramic Representation of the Great Fire
    in New York . . . at the American Museum.* December 1835.
*Squints through an Opera Glass, by a Young Gent. Who Hadn't
    Any Thing Else to Do.* New York: Merchants' Day-Book, 1850.
Strong, George Templeton. Diary, 1835–1875. Photostat.
    Columbia University, Rare Books and Manuscripts Library.
——. *Diary of George Templeton Strong. Selections,* 1835–1875.
    4 vols. Ed. Allan Nevins and Milton Halsey Thomas. New
    York: Macmillan, 1952.
——. Miscellaneous Papers. Columbia University, Rare Books
    and Manuscripts Library.
Strong, George Washington. Archival Legal Records for the
    firm Cadwalader, Wickersham and Taft. Syracuse University
    Library, Special Collections Research Center (SCRC).
Taft, Henry Waters. *A Century and a Half at the New York Bar,
    Being the Annals of a Law Firm and Sketches of Its Members,
    with Brief References to Collateral Events of Historical Interest.*
    New York: privately printed, 1938.
Taylor, Bayard. *Life and Letters of Bayard Taylor.* 2 vols. Ed.
    Marie Hansen-Taylor and Horace E. Scudder. Boston:
    Houghton Mifflin, 1884.
Taylor, Tom. *Our American Cousin.* 1858; repr. Bedford, MA:
    Applewood, 2006.
Tocqueville, Alexis de. *The Recollections of Alexis de Tocqueville.*
    Trans. Alexander Teixeira de Mattos. London: Harvill, 1948.
Wells, John. Archival correspondence for the law firm
    Cadwalader, Wickersham and Taft. SCRC.
Wheeler, D. H. "The Political Economy of the Fire." In *The
    Lakeside Memorial of the Burning of Chicago,* 99–100.
    Chicago: University Publishing Company, 1872.
Why New York City Should Have a Paid Fire Department. New
    York: C. S. Wescott & Co., Printers, 1865.

Wilkie, F. B. "Among the Ruins," in *The Lakeside Memorial of the Burning of Chicago*, 51. Chicago: University Publishing Company, 1872.

Willis, Nathaniel Parker. *Pencillings by the Way*. London: George Virtue, 1842.

Wynne, James. *Private Libraries of New York*. New York: E. French, 1860.

Secondary Sources

Amin, Ash, and Nigel Thrift. *Cities: Reimagining the Urban*. Cambridge: Polity, 2002.

Armstrong, Isobel. *The Radical Aesthetic*. Oxford: Wiley-Blackwell, 2000.

Arnesen, Eric, Julie Greene, and Bruce Laurie. "Introduction." In *Labor Histories: Class, Politics, and the Working-Class Experience*, ed. Arnesen et al., 1–15. Urbana: University of Illinois Press, 1998.

Augst, Thomas. *The Clerk's Tale: Young Men and Moral Life in Nineteenth-Century America*. Chicago: University of Chicago Press, 2003.

Bachelard, Gaston. *On Poetic Imagination and Reverie* [1971]. Trans. Collette Gaudin. Putnam, CT: Spring Publications, 2005.

——. *The Psychoanalysis of Fire* [1938]. Trans. Alan M. Ross. Toronto: Beacon, 1987.

Bank, Rosemarie K. *Theatre Culture in America, 1825–1860*. New York: Cambridge University Press, 2007.

Bann, Stephen. *Parallel Lines: Printmakers, Painters, and Photographers in Nineteenth-Century France*. New Haven, CT: Yale University Press, 2001.

Barthes, Roland. *Camera Lucida: Reflections on Photography*. Trans. Richard Howard. New York: Hill and Wang, 1981.

——. "Rhetoric of the Image." In *Classic Essays on Photography*, ed. Alan Trachtenberg, 269–85. New Haven, CT: Leete's Island, 1980.

Bataille, Georges. *Erotism: Death and Sensuality*. Trans. Mary Dalwood. San Francisco: City Lights, 1986.

Baudrillard, Jean. *Simulations*. Trans. Paul Foss. New York:
    Semiotexte, 1983.

Beckert, Sven. *The Monied Metropolis: New York City and the
    Consolidation of the American Bourgeoisie, 1850–1896*. New
    York: Cambridge University Press, 2001.

Beecher, Jonathan. *Victor Considerant and the Rise and Fall of
    French Romantic Socialism*. Berkeley: University of California
    Press, 2001.

Bender, Thomas. "Modernist Aesthetics and Urban Politics." In
    The Unfinished City: New York and the Metropolitan Idea,
    101–32. New York: New York University Press, 2002.

——. *New York Intellect: A History of Intellectual Life in New
    York City, from 1750 to the Beginnings of Our Own Time*.
    Baltimore, MD: Johns Hopkins University Press, 1987.

Benjamin, Walter. *The Correspondence of Walter Benjamin*.
    Trans. M. R. and E. M. Jacobson. Chicago: University of
    Chicago Press, 1994.

——. "Little History of Photography" [1931]. In *Selected
    Writings, vol. 2: 1927–1934*, trans. Edmund Jephcott and
    Kingsley Shorter, 507–30. Cambridge, MA: Harvard
    University Press, 1999.

——. "On Some Motifs in Baudelaire." In *Modern Art and
    Modernism: A Critical Anthology*, ed. Francis Frascina and
    Charles Harrison, 157–202. London: SAGE, 1982.

——. "Paris, Capital of the Nineteenth Century" [1939]. In *The
    Arcades Project*, trans. Howard Eiland and Kevin McLaughlin,
    14–26. Cambridge, MA: Belknap Press of Harvard University
    Press, 1999.

——. "The Storyteller" [1936]. In *Illuminations*, ed. Hannah
    Arendt, trans. Harry Zorn, 83–110. New York: Harcourt, Brace,
    1968.

——. "The Work of Art in the Age of Mechanical
    Reproduction." In *Modern Art and Modernism: A Critical
    Anthology*, ed. Francis Frascina and Charles Harrison, 217–20.
    London: SAGE, 1982.

Benjamin, Walter, and Theodor W. Adorno. *The Complete*

Correspondence, 1928–1940. Trans. Nicholas Walker. Cambridge, MA: Harvard University Press, 1999.

Berger, John. *Ways of Seeing.* London: Penguin, 1972.

Bergmann, Hans. *God in the Street: New York Writing from the Penny Press to Melville.* Philadelphia: Temple University Press, 1995.

Berman, Marshall. *All That Is Solid Melts into Air: The Experience of Modernity.* New York: Simon and Schuster, 1982.

Best, Stephen, and Sharon Marcus. "Surface Reading: An Introduction." *Representations* 108, no. 4 (Fall 2009): 1–22.

Bewes, Timothy. "Reading with the Grain: A New World in Literary Criticism." *differences* 21, no. 3 (2010): 1–33.

Black, Mary. *Old New York in Early Photographs: 196 Prints, 1853–1901, from the Collections of the New-York Historical Society.* New York: Dover, 1973.

Blackmar, Elizabeth. *Manhattan for Rent, 1785–1850.* Ithaca, NY: Cornell University Press, 1991.

Bloom, Harold. *Agon: Towards a Theory of Revisionism.* New York: Oxford University Press, 1982.

———. *A Map of Misreading.* 1975; repr. New York: Oxford University Press, 2003.

Blumin, Stuart M. *The Emergence of the Middle Class: Social Experience in the American City, 1760–1900.* New York: Cambridge University Press, 1989.

———. "Explaining the New Metropolis: Perception, Depiction, and Analysis in Mid-Nineteenth-Century New York City." *Journal of Urban History* 11, no. 1 (November 1984): 9–38.

Bode, Carl. *The Anatomy of American Popular Culture, 1840–1861.* Berkeley: University of California Press, 1959.

Borden, Morten. "Some Notes on Horace Greeley, Charles Dana, and Karl Marx." *Journalism Quarterly* 34 (Fall 1957): 457–65.

Bourdieu, Pierre. *Distinction: A Social Critique of the Judgment of Taste.* Trans. Richard Nice. Cambridge, MA: Harvard University Press, 1984.

——— . *The Field of Cultural Production: Essays on Art and Literature*. Ed. Randal Johnson. Cambridge: Polity, 1993.

Bourriaud, Nicolas. *Relational Aesthetics*. Trans. Simon Pleasance and Aronza Woods. Dijon, France: Les presses du réel, 2002.

Boyer, M. Christine. *Manhattan Manners: Architecture and Style, 1850–1900*. New York: Rizzoli, 1985.

Boyer, Paul S. *Urban Masses and Moral Order in America, 1820–1920*. Cambridge, MA: Harvard University Press, 1978.

Bramen, Carrie Tirado. "The Urban Picturesque and the Spectacle of Americanization." *American Quarterly* 52, no. 3 (September 2000): 444–77.

Brand, Dana. *The Spectator and the City in Nineteenth-Century American Literature*. New York: Cambridge University Press, 1991.

Breunig, Charles. *The Age of Revolution and Reaction, 1789–1850*. New York: Norton, 1977.

Brooks, Peter. "The Text of the City." *Oppositions: A Journal for Ideas and Criticism in Architecture* 8 (1977): 7–11.

Brown, Bill. *A Sense of Things: The Object Matter of American Literature*. Chicago: University of Chicago Press, 2004.

——— . "Thing Theory." *Critical Inquiry* 28, no. 1 (Autumn 2001): 1–22.

Buckley, Peter G. "Culture, Class, and Place in Antebellum New York." In *Power, Culture, and Place: Essays on New York City*, ed. John Hull Mollenkopf, 25–52. New York: Russell Sage Foundation, 1988.

——— . "To the Opera House: Culture and Society in New York City, 1820–1860." PhD diss., State University of New York at Stony Brook, 1984.

Buck-Morss, Susan. "The City as Dreamworld and Catastrophe." *October* 73 (Summer 1995): 3–26.

——— . *The Dialectics of Seeing: Walter Benjamin and the Arcades Project*. Cambridge, MA: MIT Press, 1989.

Burrows, Edwin, and Mike Wallace. *Gotham: A History of New York City to 1898*. New York: Oxford University Press, 1998.

Bushman, Richard L. *The Refinement of America: Persons, Houses, Cities.* New York: Knopf, 1992.

Calvino, Italo. *Invisible Cities.* Trans. William Weaver. New York: Harcourt Brace Jovanovich, 1974.

Cameron, John B., and William B. Becker. *Photography's Beginnings: A Visual History.* Albuquerque: University of New Mexico Press, 1989.

Caldwell, Mark. *New York Night: The Mystique and Its History.* New York: Scribner, 2005.

Cameron, Sharon. *Thinking in Henry James.* Chicago: University of Chicago Press, 1991.

Capper, Charles. *Margaret Fuller: An American Romantic Life. Vol. 2: The Public Years.* New York: Oxford University Press, 2007.

Carnegy, Patrick. *Wagner and the Art of the Theatre.* New Haven, CT: Yale University Press, 2006.

Carver, Terrell. "Imagery/Writing, Imagination/Politics: Reading Marx through the *Eighteenth Brumaire.*" In *Marx's Eighteenth Brumaire: (Post)modern Interpretations*, ed. Mark Cowling and James Martin, 113–28. London: Pluto, 2002.

Castells, Manuel. *The City and the Grassroots: A Cross-Cultural Theory of Urban Social Movements.* Berkeley: University of California Press, 1983.

Castiglia, Christopher, and Russ Castronovo. "Preface: A 'Hive of Subtlety': Aesthetics and the End(s) of Cultural Studies." *American Literature* 76, no. 3 (September 2004): 423–35.

Castronovo, Russ. *Beautiful Democracy: Aesthetics and Anarchy in a Global Era.* Chicago: University of Chicago Press, 2007.

Certeau, Michel de. "Walking in the City." In *The Practice of Everyday Life*, trans. Steven F. Rendall, 91–110. Berkeley: University of California Press, 1984.

Chevalier, Louis. *Laboring Classes and Dangerous Classes in Paris during the First Half of the Nineteenth Century.* Trans. Frank Jellinek. 1958; repr. New York: H. Fertig, 1973.

Chevigny, Bell Gale. "To the Edges of Ideology: Margaret Fuller's Centrifugal Evolution." *American Quarterly* 38 (Summer 1986): 173–201.

City Images: Perspectives from Literature, Philosophy, and Film.
    Ed. Mary Ann Caws. 1991; repr. New York: Routledge, 2013.

Clark, T. J. *The Absolute Bourgeois: Artists and Politics in France,*
    1848–1851. Berkeley: University of California Press, 1999.

Cohen, Michael C. *The Social Lives of Poems in Nineteenth-*
    Century America. Philadelphia: University of Pennsylvania
    Press, 2015.

Conron, John. *American Picturesque.* University Park: Penn State
    University Press, 2000.

Cook, James W. *The Arts of Deception: Playing with Fraud in the*
    Age of Barnum. Cambridge, MA: Harvard University Press,
    2001.

Cook, Sylvia Jenkins. *Working Women, Literary Ladies: The*
    Industrial Revolution and Female Aspiration. New York:
    Oxford University Press, 2008.

Cott, Nancy. *The Bonds of Womanhood: "Woman's Sphere" in*
    New England, 1780–1835. New Haven, CT: Yale University
    Press, 1977.

Couperie, Pierre. *Paris through the Ages: An Illustrated Historical*
    Atlas of Urbanism and Architecture. New York: G. Braziller,
    1971.

Crary, Jonathan. *Suspensions of Perception: Attention, Spectacle,*
    and Modern Culture. Cambridge, MA: MIT Press, 1999.
    ——— . *Techniques of the Observer: On Vision and Modernity in*
    the Nineteenth Century. Cambridge, MA: MIT Press, 1990.

Curti, Merle. "Impact of the Revolutions of 1848 on American
    Thought." *Proceedings of the American Philosophical Society*
    93, no. 3 (June 1949): 209–15.

Curtis, Eugene N. "American Opinion of the French
    Nineteenth-Century Revolutions." *American Historical Review*
    29 (January 1924): 249–70.

Daly, Nicholas. *The Demographic Imagination and the*
    Nineteenth-Century City: Paris, London, New York.
    Cambridge: Cambridge University Press, 2015.

Darnton, Robert. *The Great Cat Massacre and Other Episodes in*
    French Cultural History. New York: Basic Books, 1984.

Davis, Theo. *Formalism, Experience, and the Making of American Literature in the Nineteenth Century.* New York: Cambridge University Press, 2007.

Denning, Michael. *The Cultural Front: The Laboring of American Culture in the Twentieth Century.* London: Verso: 1997.

———. *Mechanic Accents: Dime Novels and Working-Class Culture in America.* London: Verso, 1987.

Dewey, John. *Art as Experience.* 1934; repr. New York: Penguin, 2005.

Dinius, Marcy J. *The Camera and the Press: American Visual and Print Culture in the Age of the Daguerreotype.* Philadelphia: University of Pennsylvania Press, 2012.

Domosh, Mona. *Invented Cities: The Creation of Landscape in Nineteenth-Century New York and Boston.* New Haven, CT: Yale University Press, 1996.

Donald, James. "This, Here, Now: Imagining the Modern City." In *Imagining Cities: Scripts, Signs, Memories,* ed. Sallie Westwood and John Williams, 179–99. New York: Routledge, 1997.

Dunn, Waldo Hillary. *The Life of Donald G. Mitchell, Ik Marvel.* New York: Charles Scribner's Sons, 1922.

Eagleton, Terry. *The Ideology of the Aesthetic.* Oxford: Blackwell, 1990.

Eco, Umberto. *The Role of the Reader.* Bloomington: Indiana University Press, 1979.

Eiland, Howard, and Michael W. Jennings. *Walter Benjamin: A Critical Life.* Cambridge, MA: Belknap Press of Harvard University Press, 2014.

Ellin, Nan. *Postmodern Urbanism.* Oxford: Blackwell, 1996.

Ernest, John. "Revolutionary Fictions and Activist Labor: Looking for Douglass and Melville Together." In *Frederick Douglass and Herman Melville: Essays in Relation,* ed. Robert S. Levine and Samuel Otter, 19–38. Chapel Hill: University of North Carolina Press, 2008.

Farías, Ignacio. "Introduction: Decentering the Object of Urban

Studies." In *Urban Assemblages: How Actor-Network Theory Changes Urban Studies*, ed. Ignacio Farías and Thomas Bender, 1–24. New York: Routledge, 2010.

Favret, Mary A. "The Pathos of Reading," *PMLA* 130, no. 5 (October 2015): 1318–31.

Felski, Rita. *The Limits of Critique*. Chicago: University of Chicago Press, 2015.

Ferguson, Priscilla. *Paris as Revolution: Writing the Nineteenth-Century City*. Berkeley: University of California Press, 1994.

Foresta, Merry A., and John Wood. *Secrets of the Dark Chamber: The Art of the American Daguerreotype*. Washington, DC: Smithsonian Institution Press, 1995.

Foucault, Michel. "An Aesthetics of Existence." In *Politics, Philosophy, Culture: Interviews and Other Writings, 1977–1984*, ed. Lawrence D. Kritzman, trans. Alan Sheridan, 47–53. New York: Routledge, 1988.

——. *The Order of Things: An Archaeology of the Human Sciences*. 1966. repr. New York: Vintage, 1973.

Fox, Louis H. "New York City Newspapers, 1820–1850: A Bibliography." *Papers of the Bibliographical Society of America* 21 (1927): 1–131.

Fritzsche, Peter. *Reading Berlin, 1900*. Cambridge, MA: Harvard University Press, 1996.

Froude, James Anthony. *Thomas Carlyle: A History of the First Forty Years of His Life, 1795–1835*. New York: Harper & Brothers, 1882.

Gadamer, Hans-Georg. *Philosophical Hermeneutics*. Trans. and ed. David E. Linge. Berkeley: University of California Press, 1976.

Gallagher, Catherine. "The History of Literary Criticism." In *American Academic Culture in Transformation: Fifty Years, Four Disciplines*, ed. Thomas Bender and Carl E. Schorske, 151–72. Princeton, NJ: Princeton University Press, 1998.

Gallagher, Catherine, and Stephen Greenblatt. *Practicing New Historicism*. Chicago: University of Chicago Press, 2000.

Gardner, Deborah S. *Cadwalader, Wickersham & Taft: A*

Bicentennial History, 1792–1992. New York: Cadwalader, Wickersham & Taft, 1994.

Gernsheim, Helmut, and Alison Gernsheim. *L. J. M. Daguerre: The History of the Diorama and the Daguerreotype*. 2nd ed. New York: Dover, 1968.

Gilje, Paul A. *Rioting in America*. Bloomington: Indiana University Press, 1996.

———. *The Road to Mobocracy: Popular Disorder in New York City, 1763–1834*. Chapel Hill: University of North Carolina Press, 1987.

Gilmore, William H. *Reading Becomes a Necessity of Life: Material Cultural Life in Rural New England, 1780–1835*. Knoxville: University of Tennessee Press, 1992.

Ginsberg, Stephen E. "Above the Law: Volunteer Firemen in New York City, 1836–1837." *New York History* 50, no. 2 (1969): 165–86.

Goldman, Alan H. "Aesthetic Qualities and Aesthetic Value." *Journal of Philosophy* 87, no. 1 (January 1990): 23–37.

Goldschmidt, Lucien, and Weston J. Naef. *The Truthful Lens: A Survey of the Photographically Illustrated Book, 1844–1914*. New York: Grolier Club, 1980.

Gorn, Elliot. "'Good-Bye Boys, I Die a True American': Homicide, Nativism, and Working-Class Culture in Antebellum New York City." *Journal of American History* 74, no. 2 (1987): 388–410.

Goudsblom, John. *Fire and Civilization*. London: Penguin, 1992.

Grafton, John. *New York in the Nineteenth Century: 317 Engravings from* Harper's Weekly *and Other Contemporary Sources*. 1977; repr. New York: Dover, 1980.

Greenberg, Amy. *Cause for Alarm: The Volunteer Fire Department in the Nineteenth-Century City*. Princeton, NJ: Princeton University Press, 1998.

Gregg, Melissa, and Gregory J. Seigworth. *The Affect Theory Reader*. Durham, NC: Duke University Press, 2010.

Grimsted, David. "Rioting in Its Jacksonian Setting." *American Historical Review* 77, no. 2 (April 1972): 361–97.

Hahn, H. Hazel. *Scenes of Parisian Modernity: Culture and Consumption in the Nineteenth Century.* New York: Palgrave Macmillan, 2009.

Hales, Peter B. *Silver Cities: The Photography of American Urbanization, 1839–1915.* Philadelphia: Temple University Press, 1984.

Hall, John R. "Introduction: The Reworking of Class Analysis." In *Reworking Class*, ed. John R. Hall, 1–37. Ithaca, NY: Cornell University Press, 1997.

Halttunen, Karen. *Confidence Men and Painted Women: A Study of Middle-Class Culture in America.* New Haven, CT: Yale University Press, 1982.

Hanson, David A. "The Beginnings of Photographic Reproduction in the USA." *History of Photography* 12 (October–December 1988): 357–76.

Harvey, David. *The Condition of Postmodernity: An Enquiry into the Origins of Cultural Change.* Cambridge: Blackwell, 1990.

———. *Social Justice and the City.* 1973; repr. Athens: University of Georgia Press, 2008.

Hazen, Margaret Hindle, and Robert M. Hazen. *Keepers of the Flame: The Role of Fire in American Culture, 1775–1925.* Princeton, NJ: Princeton University Press, 1992.

Heffernan, James A. W. "Reading Pictures." *PMLA* 134, no. 1 (January 2019): 18–34.

Hemmings, F. W. J. *Culture and Society in France, 1848–1898: Dissidents and Philistines.* New York: Scribner: 1971.

Henkin, David. *City Reading: Written Words and Public Spaces in Antebellum New York.* New York: Columbia University Press, 1998.

Hobsbawm, E. J. *The Age of Revolution: Europe, 1789–1848.* London: Abacus, 1977.

Huston, James. *Securing the Fruits of Labor: The American Concept of Wealth Distribution, 1765–1900.* Baton Rouge: Louisiana State University Press, 1998.

Huyssen, Andreas. *Present Pasts: Urban Palimpsests and the*

Politics of History. Stanford, CA: Stanford University Press, 2003.

Iser, Wolfgang. *The Act of Reading: A Theory of Aesthetic Response.* Baltimore, MD: Johns Hopkins University Press, 1978.

Jameson, Fredric. *Marxism and Form.* Princeton, NJ: Princeton University Press, 1971.

Jauss, Hans Robert. *Aesthetic Experience and Literary Hermeneutics.* Trans. Michael Shaw. Minneapolis: University of Minnesota Press, 1982.

Kasson, John F. *Rudeness and Civility: Manners in Nineteenth-Century Urban America.* New York: Hill and Wang, 1990.

Katsaros, Laure. *New York-Paris: Whitman, Baudelaire, and the Hybrid City.* Ann Arbor: University of Michigan Press, 2012.

Katz, Michael B. *Why Don't American Cities Burn.* Philadelphia: University of Pennsylvania Press, 2011.

Kemple, Thomas M. *Reading Marx Writing: Melodrama, the Market, and the "Grundrisse."* Stanford, CA: Stanford University Press, 1995.

Kester, Grant H. "Out of Sight Is Out of Mind: The Imaginary Spaces of Postindustrial Culture." *Social Text* 35 (Summer 1993): 72–92.

Knapp, Steven. *Literary Interest: The Limits of Anti-Formalism.* Cambridge, MA: Harvard University Press, 1993.

Koepnick, Lutz. "Reading on the Move." *PMLA* 128, no. 1 (January 2013): 232–37.

LaCapra, Dominick. *Rethinking Intellectual History: Texts, Contexts, Language.* Ithaca, NY: Cornell University Press, 1983.

Lane, Roger. "Urbanization and Criminal Violence in the Nineteenth Century: Massachusetts as a Test Case." In *The History of Violence in America*, ed. Hugh Davis Graham and Ted Robert Gurr, 2:359–70. New York: Bantam, 1969.

Lang, Amy Schrager. *The Syntax of Class: Writing Inequality in Nineteenth-Century America.* Princeton, NJ: Princeton University Press, 2003.

———. "The Syntax of Class in Elizabeth Stuart Phelps's *The Silent Partner*." In *Rethinking Class: Literary Studies and Social Formations*, ed. Wai Chee Dimock and Michael T. Gilmore, 267–85. New York: Columbia University Press, 1994.

Laurie, Bruce. "Fire Companies and Gangs in Southwark, the 1840s." In *The Peoples of Philadelphia: A History of Ethnic Groups and Lower-Class Life, 1790–1940*, ed. Allen F. Davis and Mark H. Haller, 71–87. Philadelphia: Temple University Press, 1998.

———. *Working People of Philadelphia, 1800–1850*. Philadelphia: Temple University Press, 1980.

Lawrence, Vera Brodsky. *Strong on Music: The New York Music Scene in the Days of George Templeton Strong, 1836–1875. Vol. 1: Resonances 1836–1849*. New York: Oxford University Press, 1998.

Ledrut, Raymond. "Speech and the Silence of the City." In *The City and the Sign: An Introduction to Urban Semiotics*, ed. M. Gottdiener and Alexandros Ph. Lagopoulos, 114–34. New York: Columbia University Press, 1986.

Lefebvre, Henri. *The Production of Space*. Trans. Donald Nicholson-Smith. 1974. repr. Oxford: Blackwell, 1991.

———. *La révolution urbaine*. Paris: Gallimard, 1970.

Lehan, Richard. *The City in Literature: An Intellectual and Cultural History*. Berkeley: University of California Press, 1998.

Lentricchia, Frank. *After the New Criticism*. Chicago: University of Chicago Press, 1981.

———. *Criticism and Social Change*. 1983; repr. Chicago: University of Chicago Press, 1985.

Levin, David Michael. *The Philosopher's Gaze: Modernity in the Shadows of Enlightenment*. Berkeley: University of California Press, 1999.

Levine, Caroline. *Forms: Whole, Rhythm, Hierarchy, Network*. Princeton, NJ: Princeton University Press, 2015.

Levinson, Marjorie. "What Is New Formalism?" *PMLA* 122, no. 2 (March 2007): 558–69.

Lindstrom, Diane. "Economic Structure, Demographic Change, and Income Inequality in Antebellum New York." In *Power, Culture, and Place: Essays on New York City*, ed. John Hull Mollenkopf, 3–23. New York: Russell Sage Foundation, 1988.

Loesberg, Jonathan. *A Return to Aesthetics*. Stanford, CA: Stanford University Press, 2005.

Lofland, Lyn. *A World of Strangers: Order and Action in Urban Public Space*. New York: Basic Books, 1973.

Lott, Eric. *Love and Theft: Blackface Minstrelsy and the American Working Class*. New York: Oxford University Press, 1995.

Loughran, Trish. "The Romance of Classlessness: A Response to Thomas Augst." *American Literary History* 19, no. 2 (Summer 2007): 324–28.

Loyer, François. *Paris Nineteenth Century: Architecture and Urbanism*. New York: Abbeville, 1988.

Lukács, Georg. *History and Class Consciousness*. Trans. Rodney Livingstone. 1968; repr. London: Merlin, 1971.

Lynch, Kevin. *The Image of the City*. Cambridge, MA: MIT Press, 1960.

Magnusson, Warren. *Politics of Urbanism: Seeing Like a City*. New York: Routledge, 2011.

Magraw, Roger. *A History of the French Working Class*. Vol. 1: *The Age of Artisan Revolution, 1815–1871*. Cambridge, MA: Blackwell, 1992.

Martin, James. "Performing Politics: Class, Ideology, and Discourse in Marx's *Eighteenth Brumaire*." In *Marx's Eighteenth Brumaire: (Post)modern Interpretations*, ed. Mark Cowling and James Martin, 129–42. London: Pluto, 2002.

Martin, Terence. *The Instructed Vision: Scottish Common Sense Philosophy and the Origins of American Fiction*. Bloomington: University of Indiana Press, 1961.

Matthiessen, F. O. *American Renaissance: Art and Expression in the Age of Emerson and Whitman*. New York: Oxford University Press, 1941.

McLellan, David. *Karl Marx: A Biography*. London: Papermac, 1995.

McLeod, Mary. "Everyday and 'Other' Spaces." In *Architecture and Feminism*, ed. Deborah Coleman, Elizabeth Danze, and Carol Henderson, 1–37. New York: Princeton Architectural Press, 1996.

McNamara, Kevin R. "Introduction." In *The Cambridge Companion to the City in Literature*, ed. Kevin R. McNamara, 1–16. New York: Cambridge University Press, 2014.

Mellby, Julie. "Victor Prevost: Painter, Lithographer, Photographer." *History of Photography* 35, no. 3 (2011): 221–39.

Merish, Lori. *Sentimental Materialism: Gender, Commodity Culture, and Nineteenth-Century American Literature*. Durham, NC: Duke University Press, 2000.

Mikics, David. *Slow Reading in a Hurried Age*. Cambridge, MA: Harvard University Press, 2013.

Miller, Perry. *The Raven and the Whale: The War of Words and Wits in the Era of Poe and Melville*. New York: Harcourt, Brace & World, 1956.

Mitchell, W. J. T. *Iconology: Image, Text, Ideology*. Chicago: University of Chicago Press, 1986.

Moretti, Franco. *Distant Reading*. New York: Verso, 2013.
———. "Homo Palpitans: Balzac's Novels and Urban Personality." In *Signs Taken for Wonders: On the Sociology of Literary Forms*, 109–29. New York: Verso, 1983.

Mumford, Lewis. *The City in History: Its Origins, Its Transformations, Its Prospects*. New York: Harcourt, Brace, and World, 1961.

Newhall, Beaumont. *The Daguerreotype in America*. 3rd ed. New York: Dover, 1976.

Olsen, Donald J. *The City as a Work of Art: London, Paris, Vienna*. New Haven, CT: Yale University Press, 1986.

Otter, Samuel. "An Aesthetics in All Things." *Representations* 104 (Fall 2008): 116–25.

Panofsky, Erwin. *Perspective as Symbolic Form*. Trans. Christopher S. Wood. New York: Zone, 1991.

Pinson, Stephen C. *Speculating Daguerre: Art and Enterprise in the Work of L. J. M. Daguerre*. Chicago: University of Chicago Press, 2012.

Piper, Andrew. *The Making of the Bibliographic Imagination in the Romantic Age*. Chicago: University of Chicago Press, 2009.

Poovey, Mary. "The Social Constitution of 'Class': Toward a History of Classificatory Thinking." In *Rethinking Class: Literary Studies and Social Formations*, ed. Wai Chee Dimock and Michael T. Gilmore, 15–56. New York: Columbia University Press, 1994.

Price, Leah. *How to Do Things with Books in Victorian Britain*. Princeton, NJ: Princeton University Press, 2012.

Price, Lois Olcott. "The Development of Photomechanical Book Illustration." In *The American Illustrated Book in the Nineteenth Century*, ed. Gerald W. R. Ward, 233–56. Winterthur, DE: Henry Francis du Pont Wintherthur Museum, 1987.

Price, Roger. *The French Second Republic: A Social History*. Ithaca, NY: Cornell University Press, 1972.

Raban, Jonathan. *Soft City*. New York: E. P. Dutton, 1974.

Raddatz, Fritz J. *Karl Marx: A Political Biography*. Trans. Richard Barry. Boston: Little, Brown, 1978.

Rapoport, Amos. *The Meaning of the Built Environment: A Nonverbal Communication Approach*. Beverly Hills, CA: Sage, 1982.

Ratcliffe, Barrie M. "Classes laborieuses et classes dangereuses à Paris pendant la premiere moitié du XIXe siècle?: The Chevalier Thesis Reexamined." *French Historical Studies* 17, no. 2 (Autumn 1991): 542–74.

Reynolds, Larry J. *European Revolutions and the American Literary Renaissance*. New Haven, CT: Yale University Press, 1988.

Rice, Shelley. *Parisian Views*. Cambridge, MA: MIT Press, 1997.

Rigal, Laura. *The American Manufactory: Art, Labor, and the World of Things in the Early Republic*. Princeton, NJ: Princeton University Press, 1998.

Rinhart, Floyd, and Marion Rinhart. *The American Daguerreotype*. Athens: University of Georgia Press, 1981.

Roberts, Timothy M. *Distant Revolutions: 1848 and the Challenge to American Exceptionalism.* Charlottesville: University of Virginia Press, 2009.

Robson, Catherine. *Heart Beats: Everyday Life and the Memorized Poem.* Princeton, NJ: Princeton University Press, 2012.

Rock, Howard B., and Deborah Dash Moore. "Fragmented City, 1830–1884." In *Cityscapes: A History of New York in Images*, 101–200. New York: Columbia University Press, 2001.

Rooney, Ellen. "Form and Contentment." *Modern Language Quarterly* 61, no. 1 (March 2000): 17–40.

Rorabaugh, William J. *The Craft Apprentice: From Franklin to the Machine Age in America.* New York: Oxford University Press, 1986.

Rosen, Christine Meisner. *The Limits of Power: Great Fires and the Process of City Growth in America.* New York: Cambridge University Press, 1986.

Rossi, Aldo. *The Architecture of the City.* Cambridge, MA: MIT Press, 1982.

Rudisill, Richard. *Mirror Image: The Influence of the Daguerreotype on American Society.* Albuquerque: University of New Mexico Press, 1984.

Ryan, Mary P. *Civic Wars: Democracy and Public Life in the American City during the Nineteenth Century.* Berkeley: University of California Press, 1997.

Sante, Luc. *Low Life: Lures and Snares of Old New York.* New York: Vintage, 1992.

Schwartz, Vanessa. *Spectacular Realities: Early Mass Culture in Fin-de-Siècle Paris.* Berkeley: University of California Press, 1998.

Scobey, David M. *Empire City: The Making and Meaning of the New York City Landscape.* Philadelphia: Temple University Press, 2002.

Scott, Alice A. "'This Cultivated Mind': Reading and Identity in a Nineteenth-Century Reader." In *Reading Acts: U.S. Readers' Interactions with Literature, 1800–1950*, ed. Barbara Ryan and Amy M. Thomas, 29–52. Knoxville: University of Tennessee Press, 2002.

Sellers, Charles. *The Market Revolution: Jacksonian America, 1815–1846.* New York: Oxford University Press, 1994.

Sennett, Richard. *The Conscience of the Eye: The Design and Social Life of Cities.* New York: Norton, 1990.

———. "'The Social Question': Reformers in Paris Explore a Puzzle." In *Together: The Rituals, Pleasures, and Politics of Cooperation*, 35–64. New Haven, CT: Yale University Press, 2012.

Sewell, William H. *Work and Revolution: Language and Labor from the Old Regime to 1848.* New York: Cambridge University Press, 1980.

Sicherman, Barbara. "Ideologies and Practices of Reading." In *A History of the Book in America, vol. 3: The Industrial Book, 1840–1880*, ed. Scott Casper et al., 279–302. Chapel Hill: University of North Carolina Press, 2007.

Silver, Nathan. *Lost New York.* 1967; repr. New York: Houghton Mifflin, 2000.

Simmel, Georg. "The Metropolis and Mental Life." In *The Sociology of Georg Simmel*, trans. and ed. Kurt Wolf, 409–24. New York: Free Press, 1950.

Smith, Carl. *Urban Disorder and the Shape of Belief.* Chicago: University of Chicago Press, 1995.

Smith, Shawn Michelle. *At the Edge of Sight: Photography and the Unseen.* Durham, NC: Duke University Press, 2013.

Sobieszek, Robert A., and Odette M. Appel. *The Spirit of Fact: The Daguerreotypes of Southworth and Hawes, 1843–1862.* Boston: David R. Godine; Rochester, NY: George Eastman, 1976.

Soja, Edward W. *Seeking Spatial Justice.* Minneapolis: University of Minnesota Press, 2010.

———. *Thirdspace: Journeys to Los Angeles and Other Real-and-Imagined Places.* Oxford: Blackwell: 1996.

Somers, Margaret R. "Deconstructing and Reconstructing Class Formation Theory: Narrativity, Relational Analysis, and Social Theory." In *Reworking Class*, ed. John R. Hall, 73–105. Ithaca, NY: Cornell University Press, 1997.

Sontag, Susan. "Against Interpretation." In *Against Interpretation and Other Essays*, 3–14. New York: Picador, 1966.

————. *On Photography.* 1977; repr. New York: RosettaBooks, 2005.

Sperber, Jonathan. *The European Revolutions, 1848–1851.* New York: Cambridge University Press, 1994.

Stallybrass, Peter. "Book and Scrolls: Navigating the Bible." In *Books and Readers in Early Modern England,* ed. Jennifer Andersen and Elizabeth Sauer, 42–76. Philadelphia: University of Pennsylvania Press, 2002.

Stallybrass, Peter, and Allon White. "The City: The Sewer, the Gaze, and the Contaminating Touch." In *The Politics and Poetics of Transgression,* 125–48. Ithaca, NY: Cornell University Press, 1986.

Stewart, David M. *Reading and Disorder in Antebellum America.* Columbus: Ohio State University Press, 2011.

Stott, Richard. *Workers in the Metropolis: Class, Ethnicity, and Youth in Antebellum New York City.* Ithaca, NY: Cornell University Press, 1990.

Taft, Robert. *Photography and the American Scene: A Social History, 1839–1889.* New York: Macmillan, 1938.

Tagg, John. "The Currency of the Photograph." In *Thinking Photography,* ed. Victor Burgin, 110–41. London: Macmillan, 1982.

Tamarkin, Elisa. "Losing Perspective in the Age of News." *PMLA* 125, no. 1 (January 2010): 192–200.

Tandt, Christophe den. "Masses, Forces, and the Urban Sublime." In *The Cambridge Companion to the City in Literature,* 126–37. New York: Cambridge University Press, 2014.

————. *The Urban Sublime in American Literary Naturalism.* Urbana-Champaign: University of Illinois Press, 1998.

Terdiman, Richard. *Discourse/Counter-Discourse: The Theory and Practice of Symbolic Resistance in Nineteenth-Century France.* Ithaca, NY: Cornell University Press, 1985.

Thompson, E. P. "The Peculiarities of the English." In *Socialist Register 1965,* ed. Ralph Miliband and John Saville, 311–62. London: Merlin, 1966.

Trachtenberg, Alan. *Classic Essays on Photography*. Ed. Alan
    Trachtenberg. New York: Leete's Island Books, 1980.
——— . *The Incorporation of America: Culture and Society in the
    Gilded Age*. New York: Hill and Wang, 1982.
——— . "Likeness as Identity: Reflections on the Daguerrean
    Mystique." In *The Portrait in Photography*, ed. Graham
    Clarke, 173–92. London: Reaktion, 1992.
——— . "Mirror in the Marketplace: American Responses to
    the Daguerreotype, 1839–1851." In *The Daguerreotype: A
    Sesquicentennial Celebration*, ed. John Wood, 60–73. Iowa
    City: University of Iowa Press, 1989.
——— . "Photography: The Emergence of a Keyword." In
    Photography in Nineteenth-Century America, ed. Martha A
    Sandweiss, 17–47. Fort Worth, TX: Amon Carter Museum;
    New York: Abrams, 1991.
——— . *Reading American Photographs: Images as History*. New
    York: Hill and Wang, 1989.
Trilling, Lionel. *The Liberal Imagination*. Garden City, NY:
    Doubleday, 1957.
Tuchinsky, Adam. *Horace Greeley's New-York Tribune: Civil
    War–Era Socialism and the Crisis of Free Labor*. Ithaca, NY:
    Cornell University Press, 2009.
Wallace, Mike. "Order and Disorder, 1825–1865." In Ric Burns
    and James Sanders, *New York: An Illustrated History*, ed. Lisa
    Ades, 68–137. New York: Knopf, 1999.
Ward, David. "Presidential Address: Social Reform, Social
    Surveys, and the Discovery of the Modern City." *Annals of
    the Association of American Geographers* 80, no. 4 (December
    1990): 491–503.
Ware, Norman. *The Industrial Worker, 1840–1860: The Reaction
    of American Industrial Society to the Advance of the Industrial
    Revolution*. 1924; repr. Chicago: Ivan R. Dee, 1990.
Watkins, Geoff. "The Appeal of Bonapartism." In *Marx's
    Eighteenth Brumaire: (Post)modern Interpretations*, ed.
    Mark Cowling and James Martin, 163–76. London: Pluto,
    2002.

Weinstein, Arnold. "Fragment and Form in the City of Modernism." In *The Cambridge Companion to the City in Literature*, 138–52. New York: Cambridge University Press, 2014.

Weinstein, Cindy. *The Literature of Labor and the Labors of Literature*. New York: Cambridge University Press, 1995.

Welling, William. *Photography in America: The Formative Years, 1839–1900*. New York: Thomas Y. Crowell, 1978.

Wermiel, Sara. "The Development of Fireproof Construction in Great Britain and the United States in the Nineteenth Century." *Construction History* 9 (1993): 3–26.

White, Hayden. *The Content of the Form: Narrative Discourse and Historical Representation*. Baltimore, MD: Johns Hopkins University Press, 1987.

Wilentz, Sean. *Chants Democratic: New York City and the Rise of the American Working Class, 1788–1850*. New York: Oxford University Press, 1984.

Williams, Raymond. *The Country and the City*. New York: Oxford University Press, 1973.

——— . *Keywords: A Vocabulary of Culture and Society*. Rev. ed. New York: Oxford University Press, 1985.

——— . "Metropolitan Perceptions and the Emergence of Modernism" [1985]. In *The Politics of Modernism: Against the New Conformists*, 37–48. London: Verso, 2007.

Williams, Rosalind. *Dream Worlds: Mass Consumption in Late Nineteenth-Century France*. Berkeley: University of California Press, 1982.

Williams, Susan S. *Confounding Images: Photography and Portraiture in Antebellum American Fiction*. Philadelphia: University of Pennsylvania Press, 1997.

——— . "'The Inconstant Daguerreotype': The Narrative of Early Photography." *Narrative* 4, no. 2 (May 1996): 161–74.

Wilson, William H. *The City Beautiful Movement*. Baltimore, MD: Johns Hopkins University Press, 1994.

Wind, Edgar. "Critique of Connoisseurship." In *Art and Anarchy*, 30–46. 1963; repr. Evanston, IL: Northwestern University Press, 1985.

Wirth-Neshner, Hana. "Impartial Maps: Reading and Writing Cities." In *Handbook of Urban Studies*, ed. Ronan Paddison, 52–66. London: Sage, 2001.

Wolfson, Susan J. "Reading for Form." *Modern Language Quarterly* 61, no. 1 (March 2000): 1–16.

Wood, John, ed. *The Daguerreotype: A Sesquicentennial Celebration*. Iowa City: University of Iowa Press, 1989.

"Work." Special *PMLA* issue 127, no. 4 (October 2012).

Yagoda, Ben. *About Town: The New Yorker and the World It Made*. New York: Da Capo, 2001.

Zimmerman, David A. *Panic! Markets, Crises, and Crowds in American Fiction*. Chapel Hill: University of North Carolina Press, 2006.

Index

abstraction, 13, 21–22, 39–40, 42, 49–50, 103–4; and social formations, 82

actor-network theory (ANT), 47–48. *See also* Farías, Ignacio

aestheticism: antiquarianism, 114; connoisseurship, 108, 110, 120; defined, 2; effects, 21, 30, 49, 51; European, 122; formalism, 5–6, 11; neoclassicism, 113–14; pictorial, 97, 111–13; representation, 44; romanticism, 77; taste, 111. *See also* formalism

ambiguity, 19–20, 21, 40, 73, 81–82

ambivalence, 6, 20, 73, 125

Anthony, Edward, 117–20

"Anthony's Instantaneous Views of New York," 117

Appleton's, 25, 114–15

Archbold, John Frederick, 89

archives, 15, 125

Arcturus, 21, 45, 134–35n9

"Art," 110, 122, 123

artifice, 76, 107

artisan, 38, 61, 67, 81

Asbury, Herbert, 61, 62–63, 68, 70–71

Associationism, 77

Atlantic Monthly, The (Boston), 110, 120

Atlantic Ocean: French connections, 8–9, 108; and the nineteenth century, 2, 4–5; Western Hemisphere, 23, 47, 73–75, 97, 113. *See also* transatlanticism

atomism, 4

Audubon, James, 25

Bachelard, Gaston, 49

Battle Summer, The (Mitchell), 87–88, 91, 93, 144n26

Baudelaire, Charles, 1, 35

belles lettres, 10

"Beleaguered City, The," 31–33, 136n18

Bender, Thomas, 96

Benjamin, Walter, 35, 47, 96–97

Bergmann, Hans, 19–20

DAVID FAFLIK is Professor of English at the University of Rhode Island. A specialist in nineteenth-century American literature and culture, he is the author of *Boarding Out: Inhabiting the American Urban Literary Imagination, 1840–1860* (Northwestern University Press, 2012), *Melville and the Question of Meaning* (Routledge, 2018), and *Transcendental Heresies: Harvard and the Modern American Practice of Unbelief* (University of Massachusetts Press, 2020).